TEACHING IN EDEN

Also by John Janovy, Jr.

Foundations of Parasitology (with Larry Roberts)
Ten Minute Ecologist
Comes the Millennium
Dunwoody Pond
Vermilion Sea
Fields of Friendly Strife
On Becoming a Biologist
Back in Keith County
Yellowlegs
Keith County Journal

TEACHING IN EDEN

Lessons from Cedar Point

By

JOHN JANOVY, JR.

RoutledgeFalmer
NEW YORK AND LONDON

Published in 2003 by
RoutledgeFalmer
270 Madison Avenue
New York, NY 10016
www.routledge-ny.com

Published in Great Britain by
RoutledgeFalmer
2 Park Square, milton Park, Abingdon
Oxon OX14 4RN
www.routledgefalmer.com

Epigraph for Chapter 2 is from *Field of Dreams* and is used courtesy of Universal Studios Publishing Rights, a division of Universal Studios Licensing LLLP. Copyright 2003 by Universal Studios; all rights reserved.

Epigraph for Chapter 5 is from *Finding Forrester,* © 2000 Columbia Pictures Industries, Inc., all rights reserved, and is used courtesy of Columbia Pictures.

10 9 8 7 6 5 4 3 2 1

Cataloging-in-Publication Data is available from the Library of Congress.
ISBN 0-415-94472-4 (hardcover)
ISBN 0-415-94473-2 (paperback)

Contents

Preface

Teaching in Eden is a result of two relatively unusual teaching experiences. The first involved the opening of a biological field station on the high plains of western Nebraska. The field station is named Cedar Point, but some of us called it a Garden of Eden for some fairly obvious reasons, which you will learn in what follows. The second experience resulted from an academic administrative practice that long ago disappeared from major universities—namely—throwing brand new faculty members to the sharks, a.k.a. freshman biology students in large auditoriums, while expecting these same faculty members to develop productive research programs. The idealism expressed in this book is derived largely from the field program—a time and place where all you had to do was study living organisms, enjoy the natural beauties, get dirty, and talk about ideas. A teacher's challenge is to retain this idealism in the less-than-ideal world of today's large public university beleaguered by financial problems, liability, physical plant decay, and cultural wars, yet expected to produce employable twenty-two-year olds, major research discoveries leading to economic benefits, and winning athletic teams.

Teaching in Eden is therefore both a teaching memoir and an assessment of American higher education from the front lines—especially the large, introductory science course, classroom. Both the memoir and assessment are written by a foot soldier who not only has taught in these large classrooms, but also has held significant administrative positions and maintained a productive research program for nearly forty years. The field program is the Cedar Point Biological Station (CPBS), housed in thirty-five buildings built into the bluffs eight miles north of Ogallala, Nebraska, on the banks of the North Platte River, along the southern edge of the Nebraska Sandhills. The most instructive experience at CPBS involved a single course in parasitology that produced a long list of powerful and creative teaching tricks. The techniques we learned at CPBS, especially during its early years, showed us how to completely change the character of a university science course. These so-called "Cedar Point Lessons" were a product not only of the opportunities and constraints posed by the natural environment, but also of the unusual interactions that took place between faculty and students. Not long after the field program started, I began purposefully trying to create the Cedar Point atmosphere in places far from the prairie wetlands: I started trying to build another Eden. This book is my attempt to explain exactly how it was done, in hopes that it will be done over and over again in places far from western Nebraska, and by people other than scientists.

The Field Parasitology course at the Cedar Point Biological Station, taught for twenty-eight years, from 1976 to 2003, was not only a highly unique educational experiment—at least for the University of Nebraska—but also virtually the last of its breed. Its uniqueness was the result of three factors. First, there was an enormous diversity of instructional material immediately available to us. Second, we used role-playing as the primary teaching technique. And finally, we realized that its pedagogical discoveries could be taken back to a city campus where there were no prairie wetlands and where students were routinely confronted with many competing, if not outright demanding, obligations beyond their biology lessons. Field Parasitology was taught, therefore, under what can only be described as the most ideal, even idyllic, conditions, and it inspired numerous students to pursue graduate work in parasitology, thus functioning as a life-changing experience for many young people who eventually became faculty members at other colleges and universities. If members of this new generation have access to field programs, then the torch will be passed burning at full strength. But fires need fuel, and in the case of instructional programs, that fuel is some unpredictable combination of human resources, rich and readily available teaching materials, and conducive settings—that is—a pedagogical Eden, including a Tree of Knowledge.

The necessary human resources will always be available at both small colleges and large universities. Students annually walk into our front doors by the hundreds, if not by the thousands. Most of these young people are just waiting to be inspired, most will change majors two or three times during their academic careers, and all will experience a world whose technological, social, and political challenges cannot be known even a decade in advance. Yet among the crowd of nineteen-year-olds on the nation's campus sidewalks are some people who eventually will be making decisions that shape the lives of millions, if not billions, of other humans. These kids need a "field program." I don't know if I am the person to supply that educational paradise, but I've lived and worked in one now for over a quarter century, and have seen the results. It's time to pass along the tricks we learned in that setting in hopes that someone will be able to use them in places far removed from the prairie wetlands where they were revealed.

Finally, all of the material in *Teaching in Eden: Lessons from Cedar Point* is true. I have mixed the details and changed a few names in places to disguise the individuals involved, primarily at their request, but everything you will read actually happened. All of the student papers referred to were indeed written, all of the conversations actually occurred, and all of the teaching techniques described were actually tried, usually over and over again, year after year. Student reaction to them comes from comments on course evaluations and from conversations that took place months, sometimes years, after the student and I went our separate academic ways. Any tenured faculty member at a large public university occupies a privileged position of enormous power, and those who are sent into the trenches— think Introductory Biology with hundreds of students—have the most power. But with the power comes massive responsibility. Tax-paying parents have sent you their children and asked that they be shaped into something "successful." The tools you have to accomplish this task are mostly words and pictures. *Teaching in Eden* is a record of how I've tried to use these tools, how I've tried to solidify that fragile link between the power and the responsibility that come with the territory known as "teacher."

—John Janovy, Jr.
Varner Professor of Biological Sciences
University of Nebraska

TEACHING IN EDEN

I

THE INTERVIEW

We don't see any computers being honored here.
—Ted Pardy (from a speech at the Parents Association
Faculty-Recognition Ceremony)

Mr. Eldon Novak, his wife Susan, and their daughter Michelle, all from Broken Bow, Nebraska (pop. 3979), enter my office and introduce themselves. Whenever such visitors arrive—prospective honors students, sometimes with younger siblings, and usually one or both parents—I'm inevitably reminded that my office furniture is all secondhand, straight out of inventory. The warehouse is open on Wednesday; maybe this week I'll go look for some better used chairs. While we talk, my western wildlife screensaver changes from ringtail cats to newly hatched white pelicans, to a magnificent wolf portrait, and a progression of other fauna. Visitors often watch these creatures, paying little attention, it seems, to my sales pitch. Once in a while the telephone rings, interrupting our conversation. While I try to get off the phone quickly, my guests scan the wall art—a wax model of a dissected human torso showing parasites in every organ; a Robert Weaver painting of the road from Keystone to Roscoe; a fish print (made by spreading ink on a real fish) given to me by a former student; a large watercolor landscape, a gift from a West Coast friend who flew to North Platte, Nebraska, then rented a four-wheel drive in order to reach an isolated headwater spring so she could paint the scene from life. I promise to call someone back and hang up. We return to the subject at hand: why this particular high school senior, who grew up on the bleak but starkly beautiful northern prairies, and has a composite ACT score of 35, should come to the University of Nebraska instead of Harvard, Southern Cal, Stanford, or Baylor.

Baylor? Warm and safe. Sleet hits the window. We talk briefly about the weather. In the grain belt, conversations that fail to mention the weather are somehow unfinished. Then I return to my sales job, selling my institution, my department, and a major in biological sciences. From somewhere two floors down comes the sound of construction. Did I remember to sweep up that large dead roach from the hallway before these people arrived? Probably not. We don't notice the roaches much anymore unless they're in our coffee cups. This is, after all, a *biology* building. But why UNL instead of Southern Cal or Baylor?

"The institution itself makes far less difference than what a student does after he or she arrives." I pass along hackneyed standard wisdom that seems to sink in so rarely, yet is embedded deeply in my brain from one conversation with my own son, a fifth-year philosophy major and certainly no honors student. At the time, I was on a committee charged with designing the university's Comprehensive Education Program, an exercise in unabated idealism. If this program could be put into place, then every student, not just arts and sciences majors, but *every single student*—business, engineering, teachers, agronomy—would indeed write papers, struggle with intellectual controversy, speak up in class, and encounter diversity in the most academic-political sense of the word. The committee was on a retreat at a local scenic state park lodge, an all-day session to hammer out details of our final recommendations to the chancellor. The student representative to the group was president of the student body, a business major, and heir to the state Republican political machine.

At lunch, this young man claimed he had just written his first paper—a two-pager—as a senior. Later, throughout the afternoon, I was unable to get that claim out of my mind; it kept me awake during the typical drawn-out sessions punctuated only by more coffee and more cookies. This future leader had evidently gotten through three and a half years at my institution without writing a single paper. A few days later I asked our resident philosopher how many papers he'd written.

"In English? Or in philosophy?" my son countered with his own questions. It seems there were two file drawers of such papers, many of them long discourses on some idea, assertion, or piece of literature. He launched into a list of what these papers were about, who had asked him to write them, and what various faculty members had said about them in the end. At that point I changed my recruiting advice to potential honors students and their parents, such as the Novaks from Broken Bow now sitting in my office. I knew Michelle would get into medical school, or for that matter, anywhere else in life she chose to go. For students with such high standardized test scores, so many doors suddenly swing open that it's easy to lose sight of major opportunities in one's immediate environment.

"Talk to your fellow students during your first semester here," I say to Michelle, while watching her parents' reaction. "Find out who the very best faculty members are in the humanities and social sciences, the most challenging English and philosophy professors, the good ones in history and political science, and take courses from those people, any courses. Be sure to take art history, too. You have four or five years to be a college student, forty or fifty years to be a physician." Then I ask about foreign language.

"Three years of Spanish," Michelle replies softly, wrinkling her nose. Mrs. Novak flashes a quick, impatient, smile.

"Keep taking it," I respond. "Learn to speak it well. Become fluent. Spanish is rapidly becoming almost a job requirement, even for physicians. Practice it every day. Go to Spain or Mexico." Their eyes start to glaze. Would this advice be more meaningful if I told them that at the age of sixty-three I was taking a night class in Spanish at a local community college, listening to tapes during my morning workout (*¡No hay problema, señorita! Tenemos un restaurante de cinco estrellas.*)? Probably not; Michelle's mother does not even want to hear "age of sixty-three" and her father is thinking: I drove 200 miles to listen to this? I return to my make-us-look-like-Stanford spiel.

"All major universities are about the same in one regard— namely—the large numbers of students, but you don't have to be anonymous. Three hours a semester, visiting with your instructors, makes a world of difference in the quality of education you receive for your money, wherever you spend it."

That observation, born of nearly four decades in the business, is met with bored disbelief. Neither Michelle Novak nor her parents want to hear about spending three hours over the next six months talking with a faculty member, making sure he or she knows an honors student is sitting back on the twentieth row of some auditorium. I suspect, quite strongly, that what they really want to hear about is the best way to get into medical school. I also suspect they believe, quite strongly, that good grades will do the trick. But how do I know three hours a semester will make a significant difference in a student's academic life, even a premed, perhaps especially a premed? Because in 1966, three weeks into my first semester as a university professor, staring out at 362 freshmen, at 7:30 A.M. Tuesday, Thursday, and Saturday, I decided that in addition to memorizing their wardrobes and hairdos, I also needed to know their names. After all, every faculty member I'd ever had knew my name. Doesn't a teacher have an *obligation* to learn his or her students' names? Doesn't that obligation automatically come with our students' tuition checks? So no matter how many people were in those large lecture sections, I simply had to try to learn their names. And as the years passed, and I watched how my university's student-faculty relationships evolved, the names became an obsession.

In the middle '60s, everyone in my department handed out three-by-five cards the first day of class, asking that students provide names, majors, and so forth, all for the purpose of making out a roster. But one day I looked at those cards and thought: If a student personally handed me this card somewhere outside of class, so I could spend five minutes talking with him or her, then it would be much easier for me to learn names by the end of the semester. To hell with the roster; all I had to do was give a 10-point quiz Friday of the first week, and I'd have those data. The cards, however, now had some real potential value. That's when I began paying for these cards with points. I added 5 percentage points to an exam score if a student came to my office, handed me that card, and carried on a short conversation, one-on-one. I've been doing this now for nearly thirty-six years, although recently the card has evolved into a full-page information sheet.

Yes, this activity takes time. Yet this investment of time provides a unique kind of data, some of which administrators usually don't want to know. For example, although I've not been very disciplined in actually keeping a record of how many times an honors student, well into his or her sophomore year, has his or her first actual, face-to-face conversation with a faculty member, any faculty member, over that 5-point card, I do encounter such a student at least once a semester.

In a typical year, I encounter three or four of them, on paper, at least, our best and brightest. I used to send my department chair an E-mail every time this happened, just to remind him that our advising system was missing a whole lot of our top classroom performers. After a while I quit doing that. Nobody ever wanted to talk about what I saw as a fundamental flaw in the system. But I still kept a lot of cards with "honors, National Merit Scholar, never talked to faculty member" scribbled on them.

I also encounter the kids who are struggling, and are finally willing to give up a pinch of anonymity in order to get an extra 5 points. What they reveal, usually unwittingly, is that they have terrible study habits, terrible attitudes, and have not been to class very often. In such cases, the five points rarely makes a difference in their grades. In my wildest dreams, the five-minute visit makes a small difference in their lives, but I've only truly known that to happen once. A struggling student had written two beautiful papers for my general zoology class of about 200. The incongruity between her grades on my multiple-choice exams and her papers led to a conversation about majors and reasons for taking a zoology course. I suggested she take some additional English courses, matching her obvious talent with a discipline that used, and appreciated, such talent. She did. It was a perfect match, and she blossomed, intellectually, in her new location. I've given approximately 15,000 letter grades in the past thirty-six years and talked personally with probably two-thirds of those students; this is the only case in which I actually know about the connection between a single face-to-face conversation and student's academic success. But seemingly unique events can not only tell us what is possible; they can also suggest what is ideal. The three-by-five cards are a vehicle for accomplishing that ideal, namely, one short conversation, about something intellectual, between a faculty member and a student. The ideal is not—*NOT*—a one-on-one "conversation" between a student and a computer screen.

For the Novak family—taxpayers, football fans, extremely hardworking and skillful people suddenly realizing what a composite ACT of 35 means to their daughter—I continue the litany of ways to make the bleak upper midwest winter look better than stately, wooded, fall season magnificent, Princeton:

"The standard advice, and I give this to all the students, especially when parents are around, is to take both Cell Structure and Function, and Biodiversity, before the middle of your sophomore year. Then go to the biological field station no later than the summer after your sophomore year. Start doing research by the end of your sophomore year, and teach labs if you can. Read lots of serious books, take advantage of the easily available museums, recitals, and visiting lecturers on campus, and talk big talk with anyone who will listen. Those are the secrets to increasing the quality of your university education and they will work for almost anyone. And they will work anyplace." Even at Podunk U in Outback, Montana, I might have added, but don't. This child might be someone who desperately desires to be in Outback, Montana.

Susan Novak seems to be paying a little more attention; course names sound suspiciously like "advice" and "advice" is why they have come to my office.

"We've heard about the field program," she says. "That's Cedar Point? Out in western Nebraska?" I nod, hand her a brochure. Michelle's curiosity level increases slightly. "What are those courses you mentioned?"

Cell Structure and Function and Biodiversity are the first two courses in the biological sciences core curriculum. I teach the latter. The semester I am writing this book, my class has eighty-eight registered students, nearly half of whom are juniors and seniors. They've either not received this simple advice to take the most basic courses first, or they've ignored that advice. Why would someone put off until they're a senior such a basic, core-curriculum requirement in his or her major? Because someone has told them that premeds need to get their physics, chemistry, and math out of the way in preparation for the MCAT (Medical College Admission Test). They've decided, because they *are going to be doctors*, that physiology, anatomy, and genetics are more "applicable to their interests" than insects, protozoans, molluscs, and worms. In attempting to satisfy our clientele—that is, by helping them get into professional schools—we've denied that same clientele the full benefits they've already paid for.

What are these benefits? They are the rich intellectual experiences of trying to understand the extraordinarily diverse worlds of art, music, literature, history, and science—that is—the realms of life beyond an operating table or a dentist's chair. Why have we denied anybody these benefits? In my opinion, the answer is simply by giving our students what they appear to want—that is, treating them as customers instead of future presidents. We used to assume one went to college to get an education, acknowledging that a career would then be possible. As an institution, we now assume one goes to college in order to achieve a career, and in the sciences especially, we worry far more about certification than about education. The reversed polarity is subtle, but powerful. The new assumptions permeate all of our interactions between faculty, students, and advisers. In the biological sciences, departments with hundreds of majors rarely find a twenty-year-old who simply wants to study plants and animals. What we find instead is a massive supply of human resources, much of it quite capable of taking leadership positions in our society, dedicated instead to finding a specific job as a health-care professional at some level, and usually for a very personal reason.

Over in the English department, faculty members may be having these same thoughts about their prelaw students (the humanities' equivalent to premeds). If there is anything that surpasses our obsession with health, it is our pervasive awareness of the law. We are simply awash in information about the legal system, regardless of how accurate that information might be. Our best-selling novels, our gripping motion pictures, our nightly prime-time tube fare, are all little more than a steady, droning, albeit often quite well-written and exciting, examination of our relationships with the law. This background of common experience translated into a never-ending morality tale is rather extraordinarily educational. Hardly a native-born American lives who doesn't believe, quite sincerely, that he or she would know where to go and what to do in a courtroom. Hardly an American lives who could not tell you exactly what happens on a routine traffic stop, in a divorce proceeding, or in the opening exchanges of a murder trial. My one call to jury duty was so familiar—from having partaken in this free, media-delivered, education—that it felt like I'd been in that courtroom a hundred times. *I knew exactly what to do as a juror!*

My fellow jurors would never have known what to do in a cattail marsh. My former fellow jurors, however, or at least their children,

will ultimately share, with all the rest of humanity, the conse-
quences of environmental destruction, global warming, the amoral
creep of science and technology into their daily lives, the end of
fossil fuel supplies, and the malignant ignorance being spread
throughout our public schools by the creationists. In this wonderful, complex, rich nation it is entirely possible to become a most
successful, beloved, and wealthy physician [or lawyer] without ever
giving a second thought to what the word "stabilized" really means
to the individuals—namely, our great-grandchildren—who will
participate in the "stabilized" human population, estimated to be
around 20 billion. You can also become that same physician and
fervently believe that evolution, the central unifying theme of biology, is a complete lie. That is why this young woman sitting in front
of me, like all her fellow premeds, needs to take Biodiversity early
on. And do research. And get out into the field with the beetles.
And talk to her teachers. And get to the place we call a paradise—
Cedar Point.

"The Cedar Point Biological Station is the most successful educational adventure the university has ever started." Although I begin
my biological sciences sales pitch with our crown jewel, the campus
sculpture gardens are next. "Students and faculty have averaged about
twelve to fifteen papers, books, theses, and films a year since the place
opened in 1975." I watch the Novaks carefully; "papers, books, theses, and films" do not seem to be making the desired impression.
"Enrollment in Cedar Point courses is about twice the national average for programs of this kind, and the United States is really the only
nation that has very many field biology stations with extensive course
offerings." My guests remain quiet and polite, but it's obvious that
nobody wants to hear about enrollment figures or global pedagogical
issues. "It's an in-residence program, so some faculty member will be
able to write a meaningful letter of recommendation for you, based
on your Cedar Point work." Now everyone is wide-awake. The words
"letter of recommendation" have done the trick.

I reach into a file drawer and pull out a sheet of paper.

"Here is an example of what one of your recs could easily look like
four years from now." I hand this page to Susan Novak and watch her
face as she reads.

October 15, 1999
Ms. Jackie O'Hara
Office of Admissions and Students
986585 Nebraska Medical Center
Omaha, NE 68198–6585

Dear Ms. O'Hara:

This letter is to accompany the application of Ms. Sara M. Schrader for admission to the University of Nebraska College of Medicine. I have known Ms. Schrader for three years. She was a student in my Biodiversity (BS204) course, my Field Parasitology (BS487) course at the Cedar Point Biological Station (CPBS), and she has worked in my laboratory as an undergraduate researcher for two years. BS204 is a core majors' course that requires four papers in addition to exams, pop quizzes, and extemporaneous writing assignments. Ms. Schrader also contracted Biodiversity for honors, thus did writing, library research, and oral presentations beyond the regular requirements. Field Parasitology (CPBS) is a very demanding course that requires laboratory and field exercises, a collection, daily exams, daily written assignments, an independent research project, and routine oral and written presentations. In addition, CPBS is an in-residence program, so we do get to know the participants very well and watch them interact with their fellow students. As a researcher, Ms. Schrader is in constant contact with my graduate students and has full run of my laboratory. And as is the case with all my laboratory personnel, she has been in our home on social occasions.

Ms. Schrader is one of the most truly exceptional individuals I have encountered during my thirty-six years at UNL. She is extremely capable and thorough, thoughtful, insightful, disciplined, and intelligent. Her research project is a very unusual one involving the observed host specificity of platyhelminth ectoparasites on minnows in parts of the Salt Valley watershed surrounding Lincoln, Nebraska. The project addresses the stability of host-parasite relationships in an ever-changing physical environment. This research turned out to be far more time-consuming than either of us realized in the beginning and Ms. Schrader had to scale back some of her original plans. However, she has turned out an excellent piece of work that has potential not only for being published, but also for being an important publication. Her presentation at the regional parasitology meeting last spring was very well received and she handled questions from senior scientists easily. Most of the significance of this work is to be found in the ideas that Ms. Schrader brought to the project. She has pursued this research with professional-level dedication; she handles the literature easily; and, her data analysis skills have progressed steadily.

Personally, Ms. Schrader is completely trustworthy, dignified, and articulate. These traits have been evident in her position as a teaching assistant in BS101, where she has full responsibility for two laboratories. She treats her students with respect and they respond accordingly. In summary, Ms. Schrader is a truly unusual individual who I would trust completely as a family physician. I strongly encourage her admission.

Sincerely,
John Janovy, Jr.
Varner Prof Biol Sci

"This person did all the things I'm telling you about," I continue. "She went to the field station between her freshman and sophomore year. She started doing research near the end of her sophomore year. She taught labs as a junior and senior. She submitted a scientific paper for publication in a leading journal." Susan Novak hands the letter to Michelle. Eldon watches the interactions between his wife and daughter; I get the impression he's remembering Michelle as a barrel racer or volleyball player, and having some trouble envisioning her as a surgeon. "Sara took poetry and fiction writing, the history of jazz, and current issues in philosophy. She spent time in the museums on campus. She went to concerts and speeches by Nobel Prize winners." Susan is listening; Michelle is still reading. "She talked to her faculty members." I let Michelle finish. She hands the letter back to me. The look on her face tells me she's also trying, right now fairly unsuccessfully, to make the trip in her mind from the volleyball court to the operating room.

"It's the personal contact that is truly important in our business— the individual, intellectual contact with faculty members and fellow students." I step up on the soapbox. "Personal, human-to-human contact—with people, not with the Web, or with a computer screen."

The soapbox just got a little higher; now I'm trying to make us look like a combination of Stanford *and* a high-quality small liberal arts school. Anonymity makes a statement: the information is more important than the form in which it's delivered. But we all know that the form of information—that is, the way it is delivered—is what motivates us. People teach people. People teach by their values, their tone of voice, their unexpected patience, their excitement, their encouragement, their ability to take advantage of serendipitous events, their ability to make adjustments in a project based on experience. That's why students need to take advantage of the cheapest, most-accessible resources available here, namely faculty members and their graduate students. I've known hundreds of students who've taken that time, and I know what they've accomplished by investing that time.

Then comes the sales pitch for my own university.

"I believe that we all need to be reminded, both students and faculty, of what enormous resources are at your immediate disposal here. By 'resources' I mean not only the library, but also the two major museums, the sculpture gardens with towering figures in American art, the free recitals that take place regularly, forum speakers, untold numbers of department seminars, well-labeled campus plantings, any student's opportunity to do independent study with a faculty member, opportunities to participate in student government, to teach laboratories, the film theater program. Some of these resources are probably more accessible here than equivalent resources would be at most other institutions in the country. Not even Stanford has a Mark di Suvero, *and* a Richard Serra, *and* a David Smith right beside campus sidewalks."

This accessibility makes it extremely easy for a student to double the value of his or her university education. We do indeed have the Sheldon Memorial Art Gallery, with a nationally significant collection focused on twentieth-century American art. Six days a week a student can walk in free and study everyone from Georgia O'Keeffe to Mark Rothko and hundreds of big names in between. And we really do have a di Suvero, a Serra, and a Smith right here on campus, along with thirty other equivalent pieces. We do indeed have a premier natural history museum with three full floors of paleontology and anthropology; any student can walk into this building free seven days a week. Personally I try very hard to use most of these resources in my teaching, both inside and outside the classroom. What I've discovered from this attempt is that the vast and overwhelming majority of students are completely blind to these resources, don't even think of them as resources, and generally consider it a pain in the rear to be asked to notice them, at least until they do a writing assignment and get sent into one of the buildings. I also encounter a lot of my fellow faculty members who act the same way, however, and that's even more frustrating.

"Where is Sara now?" Susan Novak wants to know what happened to the subject of this recommendation letter.

"She's in her third year of medical school," I reply, with a totally matter-of-fact straight face as if this were an everyday occurrence. "Actually, she's in the MD/PhD program." Before I put the letter back in the file, I remind both parent and child of what they have just read, namely the next-to-last last sentence: *Ms. Schrader is a truly unusual individual who I would trust completely as a family physician.*

I get thanked for the time and assure my visitors that they're welcome to come back whenever they want to. As they go down the hall talking, I pour a cup of coffee and before filing the letter, reflect on my own writing. What is it about some twenty-two-year-old that would make me describe him or her as *a truly unusual individual who I would trust completely as a family physician?* I believe that sentence comes from some unquantifiable set of characteristics that reveal curiosity about life beyond one's chosen career. In other words, I see in a few of my students a natural tendency toward a liberal arts education, an education that I know will last a lifetime and will shape his or her reaction to an ever-changing world. The biological field station is where you see this trait most clearly. Cedar Point is also a place where this trait is infective, however, and where it gets passed from student to student. And when I saw the latter happening, naturally, easily, almost routinely, many years ago, that was when I knew I had to try to discover what was making it happen.

Thus this book, yes, but thus also the contents of my conversation with a ranching couple and their high school daughter who has just destroyed the ACTs. Many of us refer to the Cedar Point Biological

Station as a "The Garden of Eden" because for us, it has so many of those characteristics described in Genesis, especially the "swarms of living creatures," "creeping things," and even a "tree of knowledge," although the last is probably a cottonwood. For us it had become a place where major life lessons—at least the ones needed to become a biologist—were taught by experiences that must have mimicked in part those had by earliest explorers to any uninhabited territory. Such explorers must be ready to use any and all of their intellectual tools and must keep their minds open to discovery. This state of mind is the arts and sciences ideal, the fully integrated educational experience that directs your mental endeavors for as long as you live.

If that state of mind could be produced simply by going to western Nebraska, I reasoned, then surely it could also be produced back in the city, even in the large, sterile, auditorium where I meet with 230 freshmen three hours a week. If Cedar Point truly was a metaphorical Garden of Eden, then we should ask what factors made it function as such. If I could step back from the Field Parasitology course I teach, and from the whole field station experience, and discover what these students were actually doing, then there was hope that the ideal could be accomplished in less-than-ideal places. The chapters that follow contain not only my description of the attempt to transport Eden 286 miles east of Cedar Point, but also my assessment of the results. Two hundred and eighty-six miles is not very far, and I'm reasonably convinced that we didn't fail completely. I'm also more than reasonably convinced that if we can "move" the elements of an intellectual environment across Nebraska, then we can move and assemble them anywhere.

2

THE CEDAR POINT EXPERIMENT

Ray, people will come, Ray. They'll come . . . for reasons they can't even fathom. . . . People will most definitely come.
—Terence Mann (dialogue from *Field of Dreams*)

One day in 1974, Roger Macklem, a graduate student in secondary education at the University of Nebraska went to a teacher's workshop hosted by Doane College. Doane is a small Methodist liberal arts school in Crete, Nebraska, and the Doane administration had a close relationship with one of its wealthy alumna, a Mrs. Robert (Clarice) Goodall. Although she couldn't have known it at the time, Mrs. Goodall had something years earlier that would figure prominently in the development of Eden. The teacher's workshop was held at a former, and vacant, Girl Scout camp north of Ogallala, Nebraska. Roger Macklem was also enrolled in a limnology course taught by Dr. Gary Hergenrader, a young faculty member at the University of Nebraska in Lincoln. Roger told Hergenrader about this Girl Scout camp, built into the scenic bluffs along the south shore of Lake Keystone, a wide place in the North Platte River, created by an irrigation diversion dam. Hergenrader contacted Myrna and Burdett Gainsforth, the Ogallala couple whose family had originally donated the land for Cedar Point Camp, asked if he could inspect the place. He subsequently arranged for D. B. (Woody) Varner, then chancellor, Max Larsen, Dean of Arts and Sciences, and Mike Daly, Director of the School of Biological Sciences, to meet with the Gainsforths and talk about leasing the facilities for use as a biological station.

Gary Hergenrader was part of a group of young faculty members who had spent time in field programs during their graduate student days, and knew from firsthand experience the value of field courses. Within a few months UNL had leased Cedar Point for five years for the purpose of starting a similar program, and one of the most visionary, grand, pedagogical adventures the university had ever attempted was under way. What Gary Hergenrader needed most, however, were some faculty volunteers and a few students. In accordance with the now-famous movie line about people coming if you build something, both teachers and a courageous group of students appeared. The first faculty members who volunteered to staff Cedar Point were flown in a small plane out to western Nebraska, then driven north by Myrna Gainsforth to inspect the place. It was March, the bleakest time in the northern Great Plains. We took a tour of the buildings, then chose our housing, seeing only potential and not the immediate reality. Later, in June, when our wives saw the place for the first time, some cringed and others cried. Before that first summer was over, however, everyone was hooked. The end-of-summer tears became known as the Ogallala Blues.

The first three courses ever taught at what was now being called the Cedar Point Biological Station, or CPBS, were Protozoology, Helminthology, and Ichthyology. I was the protozoology instructor, Brent Nickol taught helminthology, and John Lynch taught ichthyology. The first class session ever taught was in protozoology. I lectured for thirty minutes, introducing some terms, then we went exploring in the nearest muckhole. Thinking back on the promise of that first day, I'm reminded of a former dean of arts and sciences who often told faculty members, with a touch of pride in his voice, how he'd "gotten rid of the—ologies" at his previous university. Whenever I heard that, I'd wondered just how dense a person could be and still get to be a dean. Protozoology would have been one of the "—ologies," and indeed, we have since gotten rid of it. But at the time it was a wonderful vehicle by which one could put cell biology into an organismic context. It still would serve that function, if anyone cared about putting cell biology into an organismic context. If anyone cared about putting cell biology into an organismic context, we'd be turning out cell biologists from Hell, equipped not only with the whole organism vision, but also with the latest molecular weapons. Nowadays we give them the weapons but tend to forget about targets—that is—the obscure organisms whose lives might tell us something, for example, about evolution of life cycles—still one of the most unyielding mysteries of all biology.

In 1975, CPBS had a number of cast-off microscopes, and I had one relatively good microscope, namely my research instrument, which I took to the field and set up in the downstairs lab right over the shuffleboard court. The main building at Cedar Point is Goodall Lodge, named for Clarice Goodall, beneficiary of the Goodall Electric estate and donor of not only the Cedar Point [Girl Scout] Camp buildings, but also the Ogallala, Nebraska, swimming pool and library. The kitchen and dining hall are upstairs in the lodge, but the downstairs, which evidently had been a recreational and meeting facility, we used for a lab. There is a beautiful fireplace on the east end of this room, and in 1975 there was an old green piano to the right of the fireplace. The main lab workbench was one the university got from the state penitentiary, and it had a steel top. Two of these long workbenches were brought out on the food truck the first year; one bench went into the downstairs lab, and half of the other one went out on the patio as an outside workbench. The other half of the latter eventually ended up in a 8 ft × 8 ft storage closet that I was allowed to use as a research laboratory.

Thirteen students were enrolled in Protozoology and they each got an old monocular microscope; gooseneck lamps provided the illumination. When we found something exciting, which was about once every five minutes, I'd put it up on demo on my research microscope, and the whole class would line up to take turns looking at whatever we'd discovered. There were no computers, and no Internet access, only the real stuff, and most of it exotic. From that first class at CPBS, I came away with a fundamental principle of teaching that often seems completely lost on administrators, as well as on some of my fellow faculty members, namely that students must—*must*—have the real stuff. And if you don't have it at your immediate disposal, then you have to figure out how to make it, or find it in places where it's not supposed to be. Nowadays you learn very quickly that there is no real stuff on the World Wide Web except, perhaps, for airline and hotel reservations.

What do I mean by "real stuff," and where, or more important, how, do you "find it in places where it's not supposed to be"—for example, in the middle of a city? By "real stuff" I mean the essence of a field camp experience—actual organisms as they occur outside the confines of a scheduled three-hour laboratory period, and students unconstrained by time, their supply of instructional materials, or competition for their attention. But most important, real stuff is not assembled for the specific purpose of doing a particular laboratory exercise. A prairie wetland exists for some reason other than providing a scheduled event as part of a university course. Quite frankly, so do natural history and art museums, campus landscaping, state capitol buildings, grocery stores, and original journal articles. I'm not proclaiming any revolutionary insight here, not revealing any magical discovery, any Rosetta stone for deciphering the twenty-year-old mind. I am claiming, however, that when a student comes to class hoping to get a good grade and remain anonymous, expecting exams that can be aced by memorizing a text, but instead gets sent to a museum to make enough unguided personal observations on a trilobite specimen to write three double-spaced typewritten pages, then that student has had an encounter with real stuff. When that same student then gets sent to a government building that has a trilobite mosaic in the floor and is asked to write another three pages on why that trilobite might be on the floor of a state capitol, another encounter with real stuff has occurred. Small wonder that within a few short years, some of us started taking home to the city those lessons we'd learned at Cedar Point.

The existence of Eden's original thirty-three-acre spot was due largely to serendipity. Late in the nineteenth century, for some reason now lost in history, a young Mr. Silas P. Gainsforth was taken by his family to a place called Holdrege, Nebraska. Holdrege is still a rather out-of-the-way spot embedded deeply in the continent's North Central Steppe ecoregion, but today it boasts an economic troll, the corporate offices of the Central Nebraska Public Power and Irrigation District. Had any of us been in Holdrege back in the 1890s, however, it is entirely possible that we might have detected some vibrations portending a protracted battle over water rights, which still drags prairie states' attorney generals into Federal courts. Why might we suspect this to be the case? Because of Gainsforth's history. Silas Gainsforth eventually left Holdrege to attend dental school at Northwestern University, graduating in 1900. He set up a practice in Boise, Idaho, but when his parents became ill ten years later, he returned to Holdrege. According to Myrna Gainsforth, S. P.'s surviv-

ing daughter-in-law, Silas "learned there was homestead land available north of Ogallala on the North Platte River." What kind of a
connection might there have been between Holdrege, Nebraska, and
the verdant North Platte River Valley 110 miles to the northwest in
1911? It's tempting to believe that somebody already had an eye on
the Brule clay bluffs along the North Platte River. Ogallala had been
a historic cattle drive trailhead in the late 1800s. Perhaps the stark
natural beauty of that region was a topic of discussion in parlors
throughout the region. Whatever the reason, Gainsforth applied for
a homestead in the valley and moved his family, including the infant
Burdett, there to a ranch. From his dental office in Ogallala, Dr.
Gainsforth rode his horse across the river to one smaller community,
and took a train thirty miles west to another, to provide dental ser-
vices. By the time Gary Hergenrader negotiated the rental agreement
decades later, Silas's son Burdett Gainsforth had become a highly
successful orthodondist, teaching in the graduate program at the
University of Nebraska School of Dentistry.

Clarice Goodall financed the original Cedar Point Girl Scout
buildings as a memorial to her husband, and the Gainsforths, in
memory of Silas, donated the land upon which they sat. What happened between the completion of these buildings for Girl Scouts,
and the first university class in protozoology, is somewhat obscured
by time and a history of stressful interactions between the original
donors, the local governing committee, and the regional Girl Scout
Council. In February of 1971, a woman named Betty Dowling, who
had been very active locally in civic affairs and particularly in scout-
ing, wrote an eight-page letter addressed to "All persons Concerned
in the Future of Goodall–Cedar Point Girl Scout Camp." It's not
certain what Betty did with this letter at the time she wrote it. From
the way it came into my hands—passed along by her husband Phil
after Betty died—I got the distinct impression she'd written it to satisfy mainly herself.

Betty Dowling's letter is filled with phrases that ring true for anyone ever directly involved in an educational experiment, an adventure
intended to change the very nature of our teaching business. Those
phrases take on an almost eternal and fundamental character when
the venture involves travel and isolation. "So—the idea was born, the

land was a valuable gift . . ." ". . . there had to be some dedicated people to conceive and carry through to final stages . . ." "Their enthusiasm for the project was an inspiration for all of us. They were interested in choosing building materials that would be harmonious with the surroundings." ". . . theirs was the idea that had opened the purse strings and made the land available . . ." ". . . we . . . went out weekends, and spent days getting ready for summer . . . cleaning, setting up bunks, hauling mattresses . . . washing windows, dishes, cleaning cupboards . . ." "Our rains often come in sudden hard showers, and the earth erodes easily . . . some road repair was necessary. . . ." "Our reason for serving on this committee was our belief that everyone owes some time to community service." Although she was not a teacher, Betty repeatedly used the strongest words in a teacher's lexicon: "idea," "help," "enthusiasm," "inspiration," and "service." With her words, Betty Dowling tells us how to convert our dreams into reality.

Those same words characterized the faculty members who ultimately benefited from Roger Macklem's suggestion, Gary Hergenrader's pursuit of it, and the Gainsforth family's decision to let a bunch of university professors and students come out to a Girl Scout camp in order to study biology. What happens when you turn grown-ups loose in a Garden of Eden? If the grown-ups are college biology professors and students, the answer is simple—they immediately start building traditions and careers. We all know why careers are important, but why are traditions important? In my view, traditions, along with their associated oral histories, are essential for at least three reasons. First, programs are built by human beings; institutions are first and foremost human endeavors and constructs, regardless of the fact that we tend to view them mostly as buildings and budgets. Thus our great institutions are made primarily of words, the ideas these words express, and the actions they inspire. Teaching and research institutions are no exception. Traditions are constant reminders of this quickly forgotten truth.

Second, traditions and oral histories tell us how to accomplish certain fundamental tasks. Such "instructions" are rarely written down. A good example of this information is the advice on how to hold your dissecting instruments and glassware, how to use an insect net or a seine, and what sequence to follow when videotaping a microscopic worm. And third, traditions tell us who we are, where we came from, and how we got to be "this way." In this sense they function like signature landscapes, reminding us not only of our available resources, but also what others have done with those resources. If higher education has one thing to learn from its own athletic powerhouse traditions, it's this last lesson. The grand edifice is built on the words and deeds of teachers who give young people powers over their own lives and on the words and deeds of those same young people who commit those lives to ideals. The link between tradition and success is simply much more obvious on the football field than in the classroom.

This oral history of people finding the right words, taking advantage of opportunities to build important institutions, making decisions to do something, and gathering the resources to build their fields of dreams, is largely lost on today's students of science. Our introductory biology texts try to rectify this loss through use of short essays on landmark discoveries. We read how Alfred Hershey and Martha Chase used radioactive isotopes to distinguish between the roles of protein and DNA, or how George Beadle and Edward Tatum created then manipulated mutant *Neurospora* strains in order to discover the relationship between genes and enzymes. But I've never been convinced these essays capture the imagination of my students. Regardless of how compelling the stories are in retrospect, they stand out as feats of enormous insight done by people who have since grown into towering figures of biological history. What's lost on my students is the relatively humble setting in which those original experiments often were done; what's missing entirely from textbook essays is the cultural environments in which our heroes worked as young men and women. Did Alfred and Martha sit around drinking coffee, worrying about money, talking about global political events, and sharing what were then far-fetched ideas in the comfort of patient, tolerant, friends? Did George and Edward ever just go out for a beer and have a good-natured argument over some obscure aspect of fungal biology? We never read whether this was the case, but for some reason we suspect it was. Somehow the conceptual contribution itself tends to overshadow the strictly human encounters with real stuff that lead to it. In a celebrity-studded world, for example, we so often forget how "... Konrad Lorenz ... in a modern age of highly complex and expensive laboratory equipment, won the Nobel Prize by observing geese and jackdaws in his backyard" (Arsuaga, 2001). This is why the traditions and oral histories of institutions are so important.

*   *   *

In the dining hall there is now a piano that was purchased in 1999 in order to convince a single student—Jillian Detwiler—to come to Eden after her freshman year. Jill is now a graduate student in parasitology, but at the time she was a double major, biology and music, and was not only a serious musician, but in my very biased opinion, a concert-level performer. Once we found out how good she really was, the faculty and staff took up a collection to buy the piano. It is not a Steinway, of course, but neither was it the old green one that had long ago been trashed. But once the new piano was delivered, all kinds of students played it. Jill, however, chose her times very carefully, and nobody got to stand around her and sing camp songs. Instead, if you were downstairs hunched over a microscope at 3:00 A.M., you might get to hear a passage from Prokofiev's *Sonata in D minor No. 2* over and over again coming down from the dining hall above. How many times do I need to repeat this experiment in order to get it right?, you might be asking yourself. Jill playing Prokofiev at three in the morning is your answer.

There is a painting over the fireplace in the dining hall. This acrylic was painted by a student named Cheryl Campbell in the summer of 1976. She also did the painting of a Sandhills scene that hangs in the office of Brent Nickol, Cedar Point's first director. The fireplace picture, however, shows a bridge, a canal, and a long strip of land that were along the south shore in 1976. Tom Osborne, now a member of the United States House of Representatives, is also one of the country's legendary (former) football coaches; Tom used to tie his boat to that bridge and fish for trout. It was his time away from football; if you said "Hi, Tom," he'd untie his boat and go somewhere else. CPBS students used to jump off the bridge after a hot day in the field. And you could walk across that bridge, along the peninsula to the cattail marsh. We caught and ate many very large snapping turtles out on that peninsula. The bridge and land were removed when the hydroelectric plant was built in the early 1980s. The painting ended up in the possession of a grad student in parasitology named Steve Knight, and eventually he brought it back. I was at a housewarming party one time at a friend of our daughter's, and met a guy who turned out to be a rock musician and Cheryl Campbell's brother. I told him about the picture, and he told Cheryl her painting had made it back home where it belonged. My wife Karen is the curator of education at the Sheldon Memorial Art Gallery. One day on a visit to the field station, she looked at Cheryl Campbell's painting hanging over the fireplace, open to insects, heat, wood smoke, winter's subzero temperatures, and said "that painting needs protection." I replied that I was not going to tell the current bosses how to manage their tradition business, especially in the case of art. She looked at me as if I'd forgotten my roots, then picked up her oatmeal bar and took a bite.

The first cook we had, in 1975, Denise Schnagel, made these same kind of oatmeal bars that first summer, and all the faculty wives who were out there at the time demanded the recipe, then called them Cedar Point Bars. Before political correctness and liability concerns, some faculty members used to have CPBS reunion parties in the fall and their wives always made Cedar Point Bars. Usually these oatmeal bars are served the first meal of every session, too, because subsequent cooks liked their historical significance. I always explain to any students sitting at my table that these were made the first summer, in 1975, prior to computers. Nobody seems to understand why I think these bars are so important. But here is the recipe anyway:

> Cream together 2 cups shortening, 2 cups brown sugar, and 2 cups white sugar. Add 2 teaspoons of salt, 2 teaspoons of baking soda, and 4 eggs. Mix in 3 cups of flour, 4 cups of oatmeal, $1\frac{1}{2}$ teaspoons of vanilla. Spread this mixture on a large, rectangular baking pan, sprinkle the top with sugar and cinnamon, and bake at 350°F for 15 minutes.
>
> Makes 48.

Cedar Point Bars are not on anyone's recommended diet, and coeds tend to avoid them because of the calories. One cook substituted pure lard for shortening, and their quality and taste instantly went up a couple of notches. If recipes were philosophical discourses, this one would end with "makes 48, but varies with the cook." Regardless of how they metamorphose in the hands of new practitioners, however, the reason they're served at the first meal remains unchanged. These particular oatmeal bars thus have the same quality as lasagna, certain experiments involving microscopic animals and protists, and Prokofiev's *Sonata in D minor No. 2*. No matter how many times you perform the ritual, the results are never exactly the same. This is probably the reason that when I started teaching an honors seminar entitled "Research Methods in the Sciences," our first assignment required students to go home and make lasagna from scratch. My question at the time was this: How could one get some of the maturity that comes from actually doing research without having to spend the money, find the laboratory, buy and account for every drop of hazardous and radioactive chemical, and ensure the mice are treated well? The answer lay in the kitchen. I believe the answers still lie in kitchens, both metaphorical and real, and not much will convince me otherwise. I'm especially difficult to convince otherwise while occupied making culture medium for microscopic beetles. The ingredients are whole-wheat flour, yeast, oatmeal, and wheat germ. Like a grandmother, I now mix by eye and intuition rather than with tools or expectations of precision. The beetles multiply like crazy.

I had the privilege of serving as director of Cedar Point twice: 1979–1986 and 1993–1999. During those same periods, I also had the privilege of serving as interim director of the University of Nebraska State Museum (1984–1986; 1994–1996). Both times were a result of unexpected turnovers in administration. Whatever value this book might ultimately have, and particularly a chapter about the conduct of grand educational experiments in general, depends largely on insights a person can glean from multiple teaching, research, and administrative experiences. I sincerely hope my comments are not considered arrogant, self-serving, braggadocio. I've just not known any other person who has held two major administrative positions concurrently, continued to teach four courses a year, two of them large-enrollment introductory biological sciences courses, and at the same time published fairly regularly—both books and original papers in peer-reviewed journals. I'm not a superman; I have, however, been surrounded by rather remarkable people who never asked for money, in fact never required much money, but always asked for intellectual support and an opportunity to pursue their most fascinating ideas with whatever resources they could assemble largely on their own.

So here is the crux of my argument about education in general and higher ed in particular: *people* are the source of our accomplishments, not buildings, facilities, money, or computers. Human beings do wonderful things; buildings stand empty, sucking up energy, and computers devolve into screensaver mode, until a person decides—usually on his or her own volition—to walk inside, sit down, and proceed to put substance to ideas. This principle is validated every time you see a football coach take over a losing team, then, with mostly the same players as his predecessor, produce a winner. Yet, it seems, no matter how blatantly obvious, no matter how often repeated in speeches, we lose sight of this fundamental truth about our business, especially when society places such value on—indeed concedes power and authority to—material wealth.

This essential humanness of our business was brought home to me one day by a telephone call from Woody Varner, former chancellor involved in the original CPBS lease, but who at the time, following his retirement, had become president of our university foundation. During some conversation, somewhere now lost in the history of Woody Varner's daily rounds, someone told him about a woman in California. He immediately called her, then called me to tell me what he'd done. The woman was Blair Udale, an elderly lab tech at Stanford, unmarried, and with no surviving relatives. Woody had invited her to CPBS, to spend a few days with students, then obligated me to make sure she had a good time. I picked her up at the North Platte airport, wondering what in the living hell Woody Varner had gotten me into, beyond, of course, making sure that a very unusual visitor was fed, housed, and entertained properly. I should not have worried about Woody's instincts. Blair spent a week with us; she went on field trips, went to the lake with students, stayed in the student cabins, went into the Sip 'n' Sizzle with the students, and generally had a great time. She returned for her week's visit two or three years in a row. The last time she was here, she asked me to drive her past the

North Platte post office on the way to the airport. At the post office, she dropped a letter in the mail to her attorney directing him to rewrite her will to give CPBS part of her estate to help students study biology. When she died, her house in California was sold and the School of Biological Sciences got about $300,000 from that sale. Nowadays, students are able to use the earnings from the Udale endowment to support their participation in Cedar Point programs, to conduct their research, travel to scientific meetings, and buy small pieces of equipment.

Whatever instincts possessed Woody Varner to invite Blair Udale to our Eden on the spur of the moment, they were clearly the correct ones. In retrospect, the fact that twenty years passed before anyone spent a dime of the Udale money seems perfectly reasonable, too, and completely consistent with the vision that drives grand educational experiments. The fact that people who are now supported by that money were not born when Blair visited Cedar Point, however, means that we have an obligation to remind ourselves where places like Cedar Point come from and how they are maintained. That is why, in a book about teaching techniques, it's necessary to tell the story of how our institutions metamorphose from ideas into land, buildings, and especially people doing things that provide them with meaningful intellectual lives for decades to come. After all, metamorphosis is not only a characteristic of certain insects; it's also what teachers try to make characteristic of their students.

*   *   *

In western Nebraska, August temperatures can easily reach near 100°F and stay there for days on end. Furthermore, since its humble beginnings in 1975, the field program had expanded to the point where the nonair-conditioned lodge—especially the upstairs dining hall/library/social space—became crowded with computers, uncomfortable, and evidently not conducive to reflective study and writing. Evidently. So, one year we sought the funds—successfully—to build a new library building, with an additional classroom, a seminar room, storage space, and computer lab filled with new and powerful information technology. When completed, the new building covered most of what had been the volleyball court. It also blocked the scenic view of a large canyon to the east, but compensated for that loss with a beautiful balcony running the length of the building. The balcony, however, was not air-conditioned, thus rarely occupied. The first summer of operation, the new facility worked exactly like it was supposed to. Hour after hour, through the blistering afternoons and hot nights, students sat in quiet groups in the library, or in front of computers. Later, midnightish, under the stars, they would disperse a few yards up the hills for hushed conversations on their cell phones. Night after night, Goodall Lodge—hot, sweaty, old, original, Goodall Lodge was dark and deserted. Nobody worked downstairs in the lab. Nobody sat around in WWII-vintage military surplus furniture talking about worms. Nobody played Jill's piano.

If there is any lesson to be learned from our pandering to the information age, from allowing ourselves to get too distanced from the dirt, insects, snails, and weeds, it's to be found in the almost surreal late-night scene of college students scattered over the CPBS hills talking quietly on their cell phones. I resisted the temptation to ask any of them if they were talking to one another, but in my mind they were—sitting a hundred yards apart whispering "did you hear that owl?" In my heart, however, I knew they were talking to their significant others. Of all the lessons about teaching that we might bring back to our colleges and universities from the vast prairies of North America, what I call the "new building revelation" is perhaps the most important. You don't give your students comfort; you don't allow them to be separated from the raw stuff—dragonflies, a dozen species of grass, ciliated protozoans on a mosquito larva's air tube. Instead, you give them lots of materials to work with, impossible questions to answer, and all the patience you can muster. Air conditioners, computers, cleanliness, are not prerequisites for grand pedagogical adventures. Ideas, ideals, big questions, time, and like-minded friends are those prerequisites.

The cell phone on the hill problem was easy to solve; all I had to do was schedule class late into the evening, making sure there was more material than could ever be processed in a single afternoon. But several hundred thousand dollars worth of new building comfort also turned out to be, in a sense, an experiment, a Cedar Point pedagogical experiment. In retrospect, we'd addressed the question: What happens to the quality of your teaching when you make it easy for students to separate themselves from the raw materials of their discipline? We might as well have asked what happens to artists when you take away their paints, or what happens to musicians when you lock up their instruments. But we know the answer to these questions: Artists will pick up a stick and draw pictures in the dirt, and musicians will sing. Scientists, however, need nature. Young scientists just don't know how much they need nature. Building a Garden of Eden in the city thus becomes a found problem: how to manufacture all the traits of truly wild organisms living in enormously complex environments in places far away from prairie wetlands or rocky coastlines. *Teaching in Eden* details my attempts to solve this found problem, establish and preserve traditions, replicate the intellectual experience of encountering wilderness without necessarily going to places we think of as wild, and produce the metamorphosis that I know can take place under ideal conditions.

3

WHAT IS FIELD PARASITOLOGY?

Why should a man look at the world through only one knothole?
—Hans Zinsser (from *Rats, Lice and History*)

Field Parasitology is a course started at the suggestion of Brent Nickol, the founding director of the Cedar Point Biological Station. After the first year of operation, he asked if I would write and submit the proposal for such a course, designed specifically for the field program, and I did. The proposal was approved quickly, and Field Parasitology was subsequently offered in 1976, the second year of CPBS operation. Once I arrived at the station to actually teach the new course, however, it immediately became obvious that this endeavor had two overriding characteristics. First, it allowed me total freedom to choose from literally hundreds of examples—an abundant wealth of biological material—to illustrate principles of parasitism. Second, I had virtually no control whatsoever over any of this material. In other words, I couldn't make something happen or appear on schedule, and I certainly couldn't order it from the supply house; instead, I had to go find my organisms—and their usefulness as teaching materials—in the surrounding landscape. What we'd discovered was a science course that had to be conducted according to pedagogical principles more akin to those of creative writing or beginning drawing courses than to science curricula. In other words, we had to extract lessons from our environment rather than build lessons from items in stock.

Thus there was no way a person could actually plan for activities except in a very general manner. Or, perhaps, the particular activities had to be something quite different from those typically envisioned in an upper-division biology course. To prepare for each class I had to actually do a miniversion of the exercise, spending time searching for sites that (1) could accommodate about twenty people and two vans safely, and (2) contained material that was readily available in large quantities. Students would then replicate my small preparation homework journey of exploration and discovery. Whatever material I chose had to be of such a nature that it could be processed within a single fourteen-hour day, could be used to illustrate a principle, and was not so exotic that people without extensive training couldn't understand it. Each class day would, of necessity, be a small research problem with a take-home lesson: testing some fundamental idea about the way that parasites lived in nature. We would begin with a discussion of ideas, continue with the outdoor physical labor required of any field researcher, then settle into the laboratory—usually by late afternoon—for a lengthy session of dissection, identification, statistical analysis, and review of our accomplishments. By 10:00 P.M., a class of twenty students would be able to do what one individual could do in seven weeks of full-time work, "full time" in this case meaning the standard forty-hour week, itself a luxurious fantasy schedule for most people in academia, including students.

Pedagogically, this Field Parasitology course was in stark contrast to the traditional city campus model, which usually involves a single faculty member lecturing to anywhere from half a dozen to several hundred students, assigning papers to write or analyze, and giving and grading examinations. Thrown into this traditional mix of activities is an occasional class discussion and perhaps films, videotapes, or slide shows. Increasingly, the traditional model utilizes some form of electronic assistance—for example—CDs prepared and supplied by textbook companies, multimedia presentations, and a variety of voguish devices such as small-group work sessions or exercises conducted off the Web. Little, if any, of the material used in this traditional model is real. When students study history, for example, they rarely (if ever) handle original documents, or have access to archives where they physically touch correspondence handwritten by an historical figure. Nor do they ever get to make decisions that affect the way a nation (or a model social group such as a class) does its day-to-day business. Yet opportunities are available to do just that—reenact, thus "live" history—could be made available, if the right people would cooperate.

If it were not such a massive violation of our current political sensitivities, for example, any public-transportation system could, in theory, cooperate with public schools to design a Rosa Parks Day. Then students taking a variety of government, civics, and modern history courses could get on a bus, get told where to sit and who to give up a seat for, just to harmlessly experience a tiny fraction of the terribly segregated life in Montgomery, Alabama, in the 1950s. Bus drivers could be recruited to play the role of James F. Blake, the driver of Parks's bus on December 1, 1955. Movable signs could be designed to fit over seats so that certain citizens could be told to sit in the back of the bus, behind the sign. Students could be issued ribbons of various colors, to pin on their clothing, and drivers could be allowed to decide only on the basis of ribbon color who to send to the back of the bus.

Obviously, this idea is a rather creative one, likely far too creative to actually be carried off. But even if the exercise might be allowed, the amount of preparation needed for this single class day's activities would be daunting enough to prevent it from being incorporated into a traditional course regardless of its instructional power. However, the cash expenditures necessary to do this kind of living history would be about $10 worth of ribbons and another $10 worth of signs. The benefit/cost ratio of such an exercise would be enormous, assuming one could assess the benefits objectively. One might add a few hours spent reading from Rosa Parks's autobiography (Parks and Haskins, 1992), in which case the costs would increase somewhat but the benefits would probably increase exponentially. How would you actually measure these benefits? I don't know. At the end of the day, perhaps teachers could do what we do in Field Parasitology, namely, go around the room with each student assessing our collective accomplishments. We never write these down, but someone could. In this hypothetical example, the accountants would just have to accept the students' own assessment of benefits: the list.

At Cedar Point, as at most biological field stations, no social forces prevent a student from putting his or her wildest ideas into practice, mainly because the subject is basic biology, usually with microscopic organisms, and there are virtually no political constraints on the use of symbiotic animals living on other animals that few people care

anything about. So all a student has to do is go find where the preparation has been done, then decide how to use what's been produced
by the natural processes beyond his or her control. In other words:
Ask what nature can do *for* you, and how you can work *with* the natural materials, instead of what you can do *to* the organisms you might
acquire. You must discover how fundamental principles are manifested in exotic organisms, then use them, and their lives, to illustrate
those principles. When the political and economic baggage is
stripped from an activity, then only the beauty and interactions between organisms remain. For this reason, seemingly insignificant
materials can suddenly have a truly significant impact on a group of
students separated from their city campus lives.

One excellent example of this situation is an exercise we often do
with ciliated protozoa that live on the external surfaces of small crustaceans. In contrast to free-swimming ciliates, those affixed to an exoskeleton can be studied in detail simply because they stay in one
place long enough to focus a microscope on their intracellular structures. Furthermore, the cellular processes that keep them alive are
somewhat obvious in the sense that these ciliates will extend and
contract their large oral membranes, continue to pump out water by
means of their contractile vacuoles, and continue to take in visible
particles and form food vacuoles, even when viewed under 100× oil-
immersion lenses. Equally important, however, is the fact that several
genera live on these crustaceans, and the structural features necessary
to distinguish these genera are fairly easy to observe. Some of these
features are obviously related to attachment mechanisms, for example the large, subcircular "shells" of *Lagenophrys* species, the short,
thin stalks of *Rhabdochona* species, and the thicker, branched stalks of
Epistylis species. But most important of all is the fact that these protozoans seem to accumulate nonrandomly on the crustacean's body
surface, which, in turn, is already divided into easily distinguished,
thus easily counted, units by its natural segmentation. Finally, several
crustacean characteristics fulfill the essential criteria of ecological
niche factors—namely that they vary linearly in some biologically
significant way, and that this variation can be expressed in arithmeti-
cally increasing numbers. Such crustacean features include antenna,
leg, and body segments. So we simply ask a couple of questions—

whether parasites seem to compete with one another and whether parasites select particular infection sites for reasons having nothing to do with competition—then set about to answer them.

The crustaceans we use are typically of the species *Hyallela azteca*, which occur in a variety of habitats. There are at least a dozen other species of aquatic arthropods that could be used to introduce still more of a comparative aspect to the day's work. All the elements of a wonderfully educational exercise in community ecology, quantitative biology, resource utilization, and the relationships between host habitat and parasite richness are present in this system. Students require about thirty minutes to learn the structures and microscopic techniques necessary to identify and quantify both the parasites and their niche spaces in this crustacean-ciliate system. These same students need about two hours to actually collect their data, four hours to enter it all into a spreadsheet, two hours to do one small part of the statistical analysis (which is intended to reveal to them *what* could be done and *how* it could be done), and another hour to play "go around the room." Usually about fifteen minutes into the statistical analysis is when at least a few of them suddenly realize not only what they've been given, namely, a very large project in quantitative biology, but also what they might actually use this system for—for example—a study of colonization rates, competition for space on an antenna, correspondence between crustacean life cycle (molting the exoskeleton) and symbiont reproduction, influence of symbionts on host antennal function, influence of host behavior on symbiont acquisition, or influence of host habitat on parasite acquisition. In other words, they could do a PhD dissertation on this system if they could only domesticate it. In this case, the "if" is an exceedingly large word. A few have tried to bring this microscopic zoo into the lab; all have failed.

Field Parasitology quickly became a course in which we seemed to routinely discover problems because what we did generated more questions than answers. In the preceding example, the overriding question remaining at the end of a long day is always: how might one actually discover whether these protozoans were competing for space on the surface of *H. azteca*? In a class of twenty students, during the "go around the room" exercise, I typically get sixteen completely different answers and four or five people who admit they have no clue about productive approaches. The diversity of suggestions, from people who have all been involved in exactly the same tasks, is, in itself, revealing. As is typical of much original science, there are many different ways a problem can be attacked, and most of the students will succeed only to the extent the problem itself allows, or to the extent the practice matches the question.

The crustacean-protozoan exercise also is easily connected to health statistics by analyzing size (=age) versus infection rates, or by comparing infection rates and types on *H. azteca* to any other crustacean species. The nonrandom distribution of parasites is a first clue that certain demographic classes are more prone to infection than others. Or, we could be studying ecology, albeit of one-celled animals. But throughout the class day, the data gathering, analyzing, and discussing, it becomes increasingly obvious that we have only scratched the surface of a large body of meaningful study. That scratch lets us see into the realm of original research, and our individual contributions at the end let us see the diversity of human approaches to that research. The protozoans and their crustacean hosts become secondary to the nature of parasitology itself. A teacher's biggest reward is to watch his or her class rise beyond the immediate subject matter to an understanding that we are actually studying *how* to learn. This experience reminds me of the statement often heard in the art circles that a "painting is really about painting" or "about art" instead of about its subject. With *H. azteca* and its protistan riders, we're actually dealing with the nature of science itself instead of—or better yet—in addition to, parasitology.

Eventually I tried to share such a perspective with my students, giving them a list of at least ten options for viewing what was about to happen to them for the next five weeks. These options (taken directly from their laboratory manual) are:

1. *As a course in humility and patience.* One of the first lessons we learn is that not all plans involving natural materials are easily carried to completion. Thus we are likely to have some class days that simply are not successful for a variety of reasons. My hope is that you will be patient with me and with yourselves when this happens, and take the experience as an

authentic lesson in biology, as opposed to the often contrived biology lessons you get in city campus labs. You will also discover that joint efforts, involving a number of people from different backgrounds working toward a common goal always (*always*) take longer to complete than you think they should. Again, patience helps when class days get very long. Humility and patience are the first two traits that original science imposes on a human being; without them, you get nowhere trying to do research.

2. *As a course in public health.* For those of you with interests in the health professions, Field Parasitology probably comes as close as you will come, unless you enroll in a public-health program somewhere, to a course in epidemiology, disease distribution, infection rates as influenced by "social" factors, and so forth. The analytical tools we use in this course are very similar, and in some cases identical, to those used by professional epidemiologists. Indeed, some of the field exercises are very good mimics of tropical medicine research and epidemiological studies. Most medical schools have for years been reducing the amount of parasitology, epidemiology, and public health they teach. Thus the five weeks in Field Parasitology will likely be the most infectious-agent experience any of you will get until you find yourselves in the middle of an epidemic or a military operation.

3. *As a course in microecology.* We routinely analyze numbers, distributions, and population structures of parasites that occupy small animals such as insects, crustaceans, and fish. These hosts represent small, patchy, and ephemeral habitats that are occupied by even smaller organisms, their parasites. The factors that determine numbers and distributions of organisms in nature are the subject of ecology. Ecology can be done on many different scales, most of which are small, thus accessible if only one knows how to use small organisms. Thus we tend to use general ecological principles and techniques, and apply them at a microscopic scale.

4. *As a course in biodiversity.* By definition, a study of parasitism involves a study of both the host and the parasite, thus two

species, and their respective biologies, contribute to the relationship. The widespread (taxonomic) distribution of parasitism means that in five weeks a student comes in contact with a very large number of species from several phyla. "What is it?" is still the most pervasive question in biology, and "How do I know what it is?" is the underlying epistemological issue in science. You will encounter both of these questions hourly in almost any field course, especially one in parasitology.

5. *As a course in pathology and diagnosis.* Again, for those with interests in the health professions, Field Parasitology can be thought of as a continuing effort to discover "who" is infected with "whom" and what the effects of that infection might be. In some cases the effects will be obvious, in others it won't be. Most baffling of all will be those hosts with literally hundreds of parasites, but that *seem* perfectly healthy, no different in any discernable way, from other hosts of the same species we collect.

6. *As a course in invertebrate zoology.* Many of the hosts we study, and all of the parasites, are invertebrates. You will constantly be asked to learn anatomy, taxonomy, identification, natural history, and ecology of invertebrates. The anatomy in particular may prove to be a challenge for some of you (as well as for your instructor), not only because this anatomy is often exotic, but also often quite specific to the group being studied. For example, you may become an expert in the structure of flatworms, but that expertise will be of little direct help when you switch to arthropods. Only the confidence that comes from "having done that before" (= learned microscopic anatomy) will be transferable.

7. *As a course in the use of the microscope.* Field Parasitology will constantly test your ability to use this most basic of biological tools, the microscope. It is to your advantage to develop your instrumentation skills. The link between observation technology and results is something well known to every practicing scientist, but is so rarely encountered by students. Development of a sense of how to use this instrument will pay off many times during your career.

8. *As a course in teaching.* Field Parasitology is designed to illustrate general principles through the use of short field exercises. The choice of biological materials is critical to the success of this endeavor. For those of you destined for the teaching profession, this course should help you learn to design studies that rely on easily available biological materials and integrate field work, identification, hypothesis testing, data analysis, and reflection on our collective accomplishments.

9. *As a course in learning to deal with complexity.* Parasite life cycles, communities, and invertebrate anatomy can all seem highly complex at first, mainly because the animals we encounter are often exotic and small. I try to help students get through their initial shock by (1) repeating certain experiences until these experiences become familiar ones, and (2) asking that you try, early on, the tasks that seem most difficult and unfamiliar.

10. *As a course in learning to generalize.* The widespread distribution of parasitism means that you will see the same general phenomena manifested in several different animal groups at size and numerical scales that vary over an order of magnitude or more. My hope is that you will learn to recognize general phenomena regardless of the scale and circumstance under which they are manifested. Parasites, rumors, innovations, good and bad ideas, pop-culture items, all move through populations according to the same general principles. All have varying degrees of infectivity and virulence, and all stimulate different degrees of immunity. By the end of these five weeks, you should be able to see common properties of infectious agents regardless of what these agents might be.

Although Field Parasitology began in 1976, by the end of the 1977 program year it was obvious that everything we did had most of the characteristics I just described. That discovery was both frustrating and exciting because it enlivened the teaching experience in a way I'd never felt back on city campus. Very quickly I decided to try exporting some of the Field Parasitology characteristics back to my large-enrollment introductory biology and zoology classes held in dark auditoriums instead of prairie wetlands. But in order to build an Eden, I had to find a way to make introductory biology and zoology courses something quite different from what either my students or I expected them to be. How did I approach this problem? The answer is deceptively simple: I just looked around, found all the biological materials I encountered every day outside the classroom, then used them. What were these materials? The answer to this question is also simple. Readily available and useful material included: campus vegetation and animals (squirrels, insects, birds); local museums and galleries; biological forms in art; biological references in literature; designs on clothing and in jewelry; the changing weather and seasons; pets; local pet stores; grocery-store inventories; ingredient labels on processed food; biological content in popular films; athletic team names; murals in public buildings; magazine advertising; daily newspaper stories; and cartoons, to mention a few. What was the major problem with this material? *Context.* It was all out of context.

Regardless of the context problem, a teacher should never ignore a rich supply of materials just because his or her students don't view them as meaningful subjects for, in my case, a university course. All I had to do was design an activity that was by its very nature educational—that is—it achieved the pedagogical goals regardless of the outcome. The student actually had to do the activity, however, instead of getting information off the Web. Perhaps the most successful of such city campus activities is the set of papers for Biodiversity, beginning with the search for original species descriptions. A typical first paper assignment reads:

1. Select a single genus of either lichens, Ciliophora (Protista), Monogenoidea (Ph. Platyhelminthes), Oligochaeta (Ph. Annelida), Coleoptera (beetles), Lepidoptera (butterflies and moths), Hymenoptera (bees, ants, wasps), Asteraceae (composites), or Rosaceae (rose family), and find the original descriptions of five species in that genus. Photocopy these original descriptions for future reference. *NOTE: My best advice is to photocopy the entire paper, not just the pages on which the description is given. If the original description is in a book or*

*monograph, be sure to copy the entire description, the title page of
the book, and the ISBN or copyright page.*

2. Answer the question: *To what extent are these species descriptions useful in phylogenetic studies of your selected taxon?* Be sure
   to use the information in these descriptions to distinguish
   between data needed to classify an organism versus data
   needed to determine that organism's evolutionary history.
   [Phylogeny is the study of evolutionary history—JJJr.]

Like all papers in all my classes for the past thirty-six years, these
may not discuss money, health, agriculture, politics, the military, sex,
sports, or religion, although there is little likelihood of that happening in this case, given the nature of the assignment and the subject.
The subtle but defining element of this assignment is the requirement that a student actually acquire paper copy of five original descriptions of species in the same genus (congeners). The scientific
journals then become the territory to be explored in addition to the
source. Because of the nature of this assignment, the library takes
over the role of a prairie wetland. Finding these descriptions can be
exceedingly difficult, if for no other reason than that a student must
learn what an original description is before he or she can start searching for one. What is revealed about the subject of biodiversity before
a student even begins the second part of the assignment—that is—
the actual paper? Anyone—especially a college freshman or sophomore, biodiversity's main clientele—who starts on this quest quickly
discovers a number of things that every taxonomist knows so well it's
in his or her blood, namely, that:

1. You must decide what you like best among that list of organisms specified.
2. Many original descriptions are in obscure journals and/or old
   issues.
3. Many original descriptions are in foreign languages, especially French and German.
4. Your library, no matter how wonderful it is, does not have as
   much literature as you think it has, or need for it to have, and
   furthermore, that literature may well have been sent to deep
   storage.

5. Species descriptions vary significantly in quality and detail.
6. Rarely is an entire organism illustrated.
7. Original descriptions contain little or no information other than structure and comparisons to similar species.
8. The literature cited section of any taxonomic paper is a rich source of material on congeners.
9. The Web is virtually worthless relative to this task.
10. The information in original species descriptions may not allow you to draw any conclusions about those species' evolutionary relationships.
11. A whole lot of literature contains descriptive information but is not actually original descriptions.
12. Electronic databases are a godsend, but they only go back so far, and much taxonomic work has been done during the past hundred years.

This list would be fairly daunting, and, in fact, considered quite irrelevant, if it were presented in lecture as material upon which students would be tested. The list is, however, a virtual prerequisite to an understanding of biological diversity because it reveals so much about the fundamental nature of organismic biology, about the database for this part of science, and about information-retrieval techniques. Finding and using original descriptions is somewhat akin to learning the alphabet—unless you do it, you can't take the next step. By the time a student has these five photocopied descriptions in hand, he or she has thus learned something essential about the subject, something that the teacher can't really teach in class, namely, the foregoing list, *simply by virtue of doing the assignment.* Furthermore, the information-processing skills acquired are easily transferable.

All this learning occurs before the actual assignment gets done. Whatever a student eventually says about "the extent to which these species descriptions [are] useful in phylogenetic studies" is quite secondary, if not outright irrelevant, to the teaching objectives. In other words, I want to teach a student *how* to learn. I want a student to learn something about the fundamental properties of scientific literature—the nature of our knowledge about nature. I'm not terribly interested in his or her specific conclusions about the usefulness of data. I will make comments on the paper itself, especially if the rationale is either very tight or very sloppy, but in essence, all I care about is that my students go through the process. At one level we are doing biology, of course; the vocabulary of these five original descriptions are part of the foreign language each student must learn in order to communicate biological information. But at another level, we are doing metabiology. That is, whether the student realizes it or not, we've actually been addressing the question: *what is biology?* This metamorphosis, from the subject to the metasubject, is not confined to the sciences; any teacher, in any area, could (and should) carry it off successfully.

I know that if a student later decides to do serious research in phylogenetics, then that student will get into the subject far deeper than is possible during a semester-long course entitled Biodiversity. That student will spend months studying the phylogenetic algorithms, their underlying assumptions, and the software for using them. Any *scientific* project, as opposed to a *pedagogical* one, will involve far more than five species, and more than one genus. The data set for any published phylogenetic analysis will be large and complex. But by the time a thesis gets written, the preceding list of twelve characteristics of our discipline's underlying knowledge base will be deeply ingrained in the author's practice and it will influence the way he or she thinks about research. The list will be an element of "experience" used both directly and indirectly on a daily basis. When you talk to this student, you will come away from the conversation sensing a significant level of intellectual maturity. And if you ask him or her about our knowledge of the planet's flora and fauna, you will likely get an answer that includes these twelve items.

When all is said and done, this "metabiology" I have just described is the most important element of the field experience to bring home from the swamps. This element is nothing more than an activity that by its very character, that by its doing, teaches transferable skills. The teacher's challenge is twofold: he or she not only must find such activities everywhere and anywhere, but also must find the courage to use them instead of, say, one more PowerPoint lecture in DNA synthesis or genetic engineering.

4

THE DESIGN OF A COURSE

*. . . we were also just plain sick and tired of having to waste so much time and
energy . . . worrying about myriad rules and regulations . . .*
—Deborah Meier (from *The Power of Their Ideas*)

Given the opportunities provided by, as well as the constraints operating on, a field program, how should someone design a course in
order to preserve the multiple visions illustrated by Field Parasitology,
and at the same time make these visions legitimate? The answer became obvious our first summer at Cedar Point, and although it has
evolved somewhat over the years, it has never changed fundamen-
tally. To deal with both the opportunities and constraints, while pre-
serving the multiple visions, a student must not necessarily *learn*
parasitology, but instead *be* a parasitologist. *Being* a parasitologist is
distinct from *doing* parasitology; and, of course, the same comment
could be made about virtually any discipline. The challenge is to decide what kind of multiple visions are characteristic of a discipline,
then build those visions into the course design. This idea is what I
have tried to export back to city campus and apply to whatever course
I was teaching, whether it was General Biology, Invertebrate Zoology, or Biodiversity. The task is not so easy to achieve with 230 students in a dimly lighted auditorium, but I honestly believe that the
attempt must be made, and that any teacher can come up with at
least a few devices that actually work.

Laboratory is the place where we customarily assume role-playing
occurs. No matter what the course level, I have never separated laboratory and lecture, at least in my mind, so I tend to ask even introductory students to do some of the things professional biologists do,
albeit at their level and within the limits imposed by the large-lecture
format. Unfortunately, the system that I operate under allows me no
influence over laboratory in the introductory biology class. We therefore find a problem: how to give a couple of hundred freshmen who

you see three hours a week for fifteen weeks, and most of whom are not majors, a small but legitimate taste of the biologist's life. They come to a large auditorium to find a date and get credit for a requirement. I come to the same auditorium determined that before the semester is over, most of them will behave just like I behave for at least part of their time. All I have to do is figure out something to make them *play* the role of a professional biologist instead of *study* biology. More important, I have to build that feature into the course design. By "design" I mean whatever a student is asked or allowed to do in order to earn credit toward a grade.

Before addressing the issue of course design for a large freshman class on city campus, however, I would like to put the field experience into context by revealing the intellectual demands placed on a parasitologist trained in the classical way. These demands involve: identification of exotic organisms; acquisition of extensive vocabulary applicable to almost every animal phylum; specimen preparation; mastery of taxonomic and nomenclature systems; planning of studies that involve uncooperative organisms; and an understanding of both host and parasite biology, particularly the factors that influence the relationship. Given the fact that parasitism is the most common way of life on Earth, to become a parasitologist, one must build an almost encyclopedic background of knowledge about diverse organisms. Our specific research interests then are superimposed on this mountain of knowledge, understanding, and exotica. These are the reasons why classically trained parasitologists are among the most broadly educated of biologists. These reasons are also the ones that provide parasitologists with humility, tolerance for failure, and curiosity about the potential of undomesticated systems, although I admit that claiming parasitologists to be the most broadly educated of biologists is not necessarily a sign of humility.

A second set of factors also contributes to a parasitologist's breadth, and this set involves the discipline's paradigms, which often run counter to those of other organismic biologists. Although I may be opening up a can of academic political worms, this difference probably needs to be explored because our paradigms influence greatly not only what we teach, or try to teach, but also, consequently, the design of our courses. There are many good illustrations of the conceptual gulf between parasitologists and most other biologists, but one excellent example involves the infamous Red Queen Hypothesis, also called the Evolutionary Arms Race, an idea that invokes a contest between host and parasite.

The logic of this hypothesis is unassailable, at least in human terms. In the Arms Race, the parasite evolves to become more pathogenic while the host evolves more effective defenses, and the relationship then becomes a standoff with each participant changing in response to the other. The term "Red Queen" comes from the Alice in Wonderland story in which the Red Queen has to run as fast as she can just to stay in one place. Some scientists have made excellent reputations pursuing the Red Queen (who is going nowhere!), and their observations suggest that in highly selected cases, hosts and parasites might well be responding to one another as predicted. Because course design consists primarily of the activities you ask your students to perform, if I accepted the Red Queen Hypothesis as a generally accurate reflection of what happens in nature, then I'd build part of my activity list around that acceptance, thus go looking for ways to illustrate the phenomenon.

Without delving into the details, however, the biggest problem with the Evolutionary Arms Race is that it completely ignores the ecological factors that most strongly influence the size of many parasite populations—namely—abiotic conditions of transmission, and numbers and movements of hosts. These factors have little to do with either pathogenicity or immunity; instead, they consist mainly of wind, water, temperature, topography, insects, snails, and bad luck. There is little evidence that parasites evolve in response to these phenomena except by simply producing large numbers of progeny and resistant cysts. The link between pathology and reproductive output is especially tenuous, becoming even more so when parasitic relationships are analyzed at the level of host population. The Red Queen demands continuous rounds of adaptation and counteradaptation, and admittedly, this type of evolutionary relationship apparently operates in some cases, especially with microbes. But in nature, most host individuals are infected lightly or not at all, at least with parasites such as worms. Thus parasite genetic diversity is not necessarily displayed against host genetic diversity, and this situation is especially true over succeeding generations. So given the multitude of opportunities for finding evidence, we don't have much evidence that such a contest actually occurs as a *general* rule. In fact, the vast and overwhelming number of symbiotic organisms are not pathogenic at all, at least as we define the term. Indeed, maximizing parasite reproduction, presumably consistent with the "goal" of all species, may well be completely unrelated to pathogenicity. This latter possibility is consistent, but not necessarily in a causal way, with the old adage that a well-adapted parasite is a benign one, a concept that has been attacked heavily by some whose focus is on microbes.

In the case of parasites, therefore, the central questions are: (1) What factors actually limit parasite populations in nature? (2) What evidence do we have that parasites are responding evolutionarily to these factors? (3) What are the selective forces actually acting on parasite populations? Central questions are not unique to parasitology, of course, and certainly must exist for disciplines ranging from art history to Zoroastrianism. In our case, the field experience must be one in which we ask how a particular group of organisms live in nature, where they occur, how they are transmitted, how they may be distinguished from one another, and how many there are. These questions reduce to a single deceptively simple one—Who's infected with whom? Ideally, the answers to purely scientific questions such as these should guide course design. But the design should be built around the *search* for these answers instead of an *assumption* about what those answers would be. This principle of building course designs from the central questions of a discipline should apply to virtually any area whether it is music, history, sociology, economics, or agronomy. The principle involved is easily exportable: discover the fundamental questions of a discipline, then build the learning experience around those questions, no matter what the discipline.

At Cedar Point I have three weeks to produce students who think and act like parasitologists. That is, after I get finished with them they would, by virtue of habit and training, walk up to a pond in some far-off and exotic land, survey it, then set out to discover who's infected with whom among the local fish, insects, snails, annelids, and crustaceans. I have complete faith that by acquiring this behavior, students will also become problem-seekers instead of problemsolvers. They will find more questions than they can answer simply because there are so many organisms, so many parasitic relationships yet to be studied seriously. Thus instead of assuming a paradigm such as The Evolutionary Arms Race, then looking for instances to confirm its validity, we go into the field with a clean mental slate, knowing that if we collect, identify, count, and measure, then we can infer processes. The problems we find are derived from the inferences. Furthermore, the problems are delivered to us in a matrix of context. We do have, however, a specific list of tasks—perhaps "activities" is a better word—that, if performed regularly, accomplish the pedagogical goals. These activities are:

1. The daily principle-based exercise.
2. Statistical analysis.
3. The shared responsibility for class materials.
4. Acquisition of reverence for dissection instruments as tools of the trade.
5. Acquisition of microscope skills far beyond those of a typical biology major.
6. The daily practical exam (in recent years based on videotape of the previous day's work).
7. The daily written assignment.
8. Go-around-the-room formalized discussion, converting the students into teachers.
9. A collection, with data handled as would by done by a museum curator.
10. A mock exercise in tropical medicine.
11. A research project.
12. Daily cleanup and burial (if required).
13. Routine informal interaction, e.g., late evenings at the White Gate (outside CPBS property) where people can sit in the back of a pickup and watch the falling stars.
14. The session-ending symposium.

This kind of list is not exclusive to a single subject and a single course. What activities would a student in an introductory economics class, for example, have to participate in to *be* an economist rather than *learn* economics? What might we ask 250 students in a first-year American history class to *do* so that they could *be* historians for a semester? I submit that any teacher anywhere in any subject could simply ask: What do I *do* in order to *be* a ———? The answer to that question is the list of activities that teacher then plans for his or her students: the design of a course.

The tasks in the preceding list are what a student accomplishes, or participates in, during a session at Cedar Point. Obviously, in some cases the items are not really tasks, but simply experiences, albeit ones for which a student must prepare. The list is also a summary of the daily life of a parasitologist. It may not be completely clear to the nonbiologist what the items in the list actually involve, so they merit some elaboration, especially because in a few pages I will try to address the problem of exporting these experiences back to city campus. The targets of such exportation, of course, include the large (200+ students) Introductory Biology lecture, the majors Biodiversity course (~100 students), Invertebrate Zoology (15 students), and the group that works in my lab. If this list has any value beyond Field Parasitology, it might be as a reminder of the diversity of any scholar's intellectual life. Each area of human endeavor has a comparable and surprisingly lengthy list of behaviors. All we have to do is reflect on what they are, and what they accomplish for us. I don't know what kind of list might be developed by an artist, or a philosopher, but I do know, however, that if a philosophy student did a philosopher's list, then that student would be involved in some serious role-playing. Back to specifics.

The most important aspect of our activity is a daily exercise in which we illustrate a principle. First principles in parasitology are easy to demonstrate if one has access to wild animals. What are these principles? They are assertions such as the following: parasite populations are aggregated; some parasites are quite specific to their hosts; host demographic classes vary in their infection rates; host species differ in the richness of their parasite fauna; life cycles are a series of discrete developmental events; transmission does not occur unless vectors are present; vectors behave in specific ways. This list could go on for another two or three pages. More telling, however, the same list that governs the way microscopic worms live in minnows could just as easily have been developed for human beings and for human affairs in general. These principles also apply not only to infectious organisms, but also to rumors, ideas, innovations, and information, for example, hoolahoops and wartime matériel, that move through human populations (Cavalli-Sforza and Feldman, 1981). I'd not be terribly surprised to find that an advertising major's concerns about infective desires were almost identical—in a very general but real way—to a parasitologist's concerns about infective tapeworms.

Statistical analysis is essential for any valid science experience. Statistics is also an area in which one can get into a morass of problems in study design and interpretation. It's very easy to become intimidated by those who are what I call "competitive statisticians"— out to beat you down with their knowledge. Usually such knowledge is focused on *your* mistakes, which makes you feel like an absolute fool. Having been on the receiving end of such behavior more than once, I'm pretty sympathetic with students who have never analyzed anything statistically, especially the numbers resulting from a day's hard labor involving uncooperative wild organisms. My approach to this situation is fairly simple: Give them the tools, make them collect the numbers, ask them to crunch the numbers with their tools, then get out of their way. Nobody has ever been hurt much by making a mistake under such teaching conditions; statistical software is not a chain saw. So one year I wrote a very simple statistical package, handed it out to my students, showed them how to use it, and got out of their way.

Sure, we ended up applying some methods that may have been inappropriate for a professional, such as using standard t-tests and ANOVAs (analyses of variance) on numbers that were not normally distributed. But remember these are people who had never used statistical tools of any kind to test a hypothesis. This aspect of the course design simply asks students get in the habit of doing something, then get in the habit of thinking about doing it beforehand. Then after they've gotten past those first, biggest hurdles, step over the smaller hurdles, which, with increasing knowledge, become smaller and smaller. Once you learn what t-tests and ANOVAs are supposed to do, and how to run the machine, then it's a very minor hurdle to transform data that are not normally distributed. In other words, the reasons for doing an additional something becomes clear once you've figured out why you do the first something. When the tools are harmless, course design must put those tools into students' hands along with demand that they be used, rather than require some lengthy apprenticeship so one can learn to use tools "properly." I am always amazed at how often the apprenticeship approach is used to sustain a faculty member's dominance over students. Conversely, I am equally amazed at how quickly naive students can discover, quite on their own, what they don't know when simply given a tool and some stuff to use it on. That is, the combination of naiveté, real stuff, a shared task, and a harmless but useful tool, will teach people how to learn every time. When you're six years old, sitting down at the piano for the first time, then the person sitting next to you needs to be patient and supportive instead of competitive and judgmental. And when you're twenty years old, using statistics for the first time, then the person sitting next to you needs to have those same teacherly characteristics.

Item (3), the shared responsibility for class materials, is probably the third most important component of field parasitology. I usually assign responsibilities in a way that violates everyone's perception of gender roles and leadership potential. For example, the most stereotypical frat rat usually gets assigned the grease pencil. Why? Because it is a crucial item of equipment, but it could be carried by your pet mouse. When you go to the field, it is vitally important to know which bucket of stuff came from where. Grease pencils work when felt tips don't; grease pencil labels generally don't get rubbed off. After a few years, a five-gallon bucket may acquire a history of class collections. We also tend to find out that the stereotypical obnoxious frat rat is just that, a stereotype that gets revealed the first time we go out and discover that he's left the grease pencil back in the lab. Then we all go back to the lab to get the grease pencil. After that, he's a very responsible citizen, and even begins to take pride in his critical role as the recorder of information essential for the entire group. I usually assign portable aerators to women; they are more responsible than the men are from the start, and tend not to drop our aerators in the river. The rest of the list includes white pans, buckets with lids, ice in an ice chest, plastic gallon jars, insect nets, aquatic dip nets, and seines. We carry a lot of things into the field. Whenever we finish collecting, we inventory equipment. The coed who left a white pan on the sandbar half a mile back gets to go back and get it. Usually people forget or temporarily lose things only once. I haven't figured out exactly how to export this feature of field parasitology back to city campus, mainly because no city campus lecture has the same kind of shared and essential equipment. Besides, in a class of 200+ (our Biol Sci 101), it's impossible to find something for everyone that we all need every class period.

So item (3) is a found problem in the construction of an Eden-like classroom. I believe we came close to solving it in the Biodiversity course (~100 students) with the fingertip plates. A fingertip plate is an agar plate (petri dish) with some nutrient medium. Each student carefully raises the petri dish lid, make a gentle imprint with his or her fingers on the agar surface, closes the lid, turns the plate upside down, writes his or her name on the bottom, then lets the plate sit for a week. The fingertip plate works beautifully because the resulting bacterial and fungal colonies are very pretty, and diverse, but also a little gross. I encourage students not to go poking around in bodily orifices before making these plates. We use these homegrown cultures for two laboratory exercises, each of which require use of an entire lab's plates—that is—everyone contributes.

I don't believe it's too much of a stretch to equate fingertip plates in Biodiversity to essays or poems, shared with fellow students, in a freshman English class. Both sets of materials have two properties. First, they are produced by students. Second, they are very diverse at the individual level, but exceedingly communal at another level. We all share a common problem (our fingers have bacteria, or how to rhyme [or *not* rhyme!] with "daisy"), yet we all have our own unique solutions to that problem. The fingerprint plate is also one of the most democratic of all biology exercises. You can't tell who will have the most diverse flora on those fingertips. Class poems are not so egalitarian; some people are simply better poets than others.

Dissection instruments are, like statistical software, biologists' tools of the trade; however, you can hurt yourself with a scalpel. Rarely if ever do city campus students possess their own tools, a possible exception being scientific calculators required for some physics and upper-division chemistry classes. In a Field Parasitology course, dissection instruments immediately become highly personal items upon which all success ultimately depends. I select these tools and the students buy them. I provide the sharpening stones and show them how to sharpen forceps. Then I give them something to dissect that cannot be dissected except through skillful, careful use of sharp tools. Insects 5 mm long are pretty good teaching materials in this regard. After that, my students understand completely the link between being a parasitologist and being skillful with your own personal tools of the trade. The microscope works beautifully for a biologist, but not until a student starts doing independent research. The teacher who comes up with a tools-of-the-trade equivalent for 200+ students in a large introductory science class will have made a massive leap in quality of instruction. Studio art and music teachers accomplish this qualitative leap by default and their students know it. Personal tools of the trade have more of an intellectual impact on students than perhaps any other item; possession of such tools, and regular use of them, makes a person *feel* like a professional, no matter how far off that career success might be into the future. I'm reminded of this rule every time I see an art or music student walking across campus; they always have their tools with them.

The daily practical exam is a direct result of my exposure to George M. Sutton, a renowned ornithologist at the University of Oklahoma. He gave students a quiz every day and counted off a point for every mistake, no matter how minor. He also had a writing assignment due every class day, again counting off a point for every tiny mistake. I have no idea how he managed to remain so famous and still devote so much time to his teaching, although his classes were always small. Professionals write every day; so must students. At Cedar Point, the daily written assignment (7) quickly evolved into the daily question set (see Chapter 7). Setting aside the deep knowledge that comes from experience, and the knowledge that great questions are usually asked in retrospect, I decided simply to start asking my students to write questions instead of answers. If "great questions" were the hallmark of a good scientist, then perhaps some early practice would help my students become better skilled at posing such questions. Over a five-week period, field parasitology students will write nine question sets, each set being based on the previous day's work; in a class of twenty, that's 1800 questions per summer. That's a lot of questions. And a few years later, when we instituted the Biodiversity course, I incorporated the question set as a weekly written assignment in lab, each set being based on the previous week's lab. From a class of ninety students in Biodiversity, during a regular semester, would come nearly 12,000 questions. I don't know whether this simple task of writing questions has changed anyone into a better biologist; I do know that I've not seen so many questions since the Vietnam War.

In my opinion, go-around-the-room (8) is probably the second most innovative teaching device of field parasitology, and one that I often use back on city campus (again, see Chapter 7). Go-around-the-room is very simple: each student makes some kind of a verbal contribution to the discussion, in sequence, until everyone has spoken. The key words here are "each" and "everyone." How can such a simple activity be innovative? The answer is that go-around-the-room is the most democratic and leveling of all discussion formats. That is, we are shown immediately that nobody has a monopoly on ideas or insight, a rule of intellectual endeavor that my post-doc adviser, Leslie Stauber at Rutgers University, used to repeat constantly. Only a faculty member's courage and imagination put limits on this rather extraordinarily powerful teaching device. Trust me, if you're a teacher, try it and you'll never go back to any other "discussion" format because it converts students into teachers.

What are these students teaching themselves? They're teaching one another that they all have something to contribute to the discipline, that whatever specific phenomenon we've been studying is far richer and more complex than at first envisioned, and they're teaching themselves what they've actually learned. What do we talk about in a large lecture section—General Biology or Biodiversity? Anything appropriate to the subject at hand. Some examples from past semesters include: What value is a dirt collection? For what phenomenon could this shell be a metaphor? What are the metabolic pathways a biologist sees in a Cézanne still life? What species are present in a typical landscape painting? Why should I actually hold this dead bird up against my cheek? How could a nitrogen atom from a *Tyrannosaurus rex* end up in a terrorist's bomb?

Whether or not you ever believe that go-around-the-room is an effective teaching device, I strongly recommend that you at least try the following exercise. *If you could put twenty-five words or less in the mouths of the world's five most influential living people, who would you choose and what would you have them say in order to make the world a better place for your children?* I tried this particular problem as a pop quiz once in an undergraduate honors seminar and have never been able to forget the results. I think about those answers every day, especially when deciding whether or not to try something outrageous in the classroom. After that experience, of course, the decision to do something outrageous is a no-brainer. I love go-round-the-room. It's an essential part of the design of every course I teach.

There is also an element of go-around-the-room that I've tried to incorporated into writing assignments (see Chapter 5), namely a specified length that goes well beyond what is obviously needed for a satisfactory answer. In go-around-the-room this quality is achieved by having at least a dozen students in class. After about the third or fourth student has spoken, then the rest of must start thinking harder, and progressively harder, to come up with an original contribution. In the case of certain writing assignments, the first two or three sentences are easy to produce. The learning starts when a student sits down at his or her computer late at night and begins filling up the remaining 2+ pages. The teacher's responsibility is to find the assignment that produces this kind of a struggle but not the outright hostility that comes with being unable to satisfy an authority. The authority in this activity is the person doing the work, not the person "grading" it. Credit is given for a successful attempt, acknowledging that if the teacher has fulfilled his or her part of the bargain, then content will be as varied as humanity, but the struggle to produce it will be common to all truly original work. Again, I use this design feature, namely that of asking for a product far in excess of what the subject seems to provide, in every course I teach from the beginning to the advanced.

The field program provides one opportunity that I have not tried to export to city campus, namely the mock tropical medicine exercise. For example, we could make up a little situation—some poor nation is struggling with a malaria epidemic and we're the team sent in to rescue the people. What would we have to do to complete this mission? The answer is simple: Find out where the mosquitoes are breeding, which species are present, when and where the most biting occurs, and write a report recommending specific methods of mosquito control. At Cedar Point this task usually takes from 8:00 A.M. until about midnight; the last three hours are usually spent trying to write the report. Depending on the year, we've done the same exercise on schistosomiasis, using snails, and on onchocerciasis using black fly larvae. Is there much difference between what we do in western Nebraska and what this same experience would be like in a developing country? Not much, with one exception: nobody gets hurt or sick in Nebraska. So I usually spice up the action by writing a brutal megalomaniac dictator into the scenario; it's frightening how quickly students accept the reality of this fictitious terror, even though he lives only on paper. He's obviously come alive in their minds.

The session-ending symposium is a formality that is easily exported, and I'm surprised that it's not used more often throughout higher education. When everyone has been working on something unique, and everyone knows it, then a formal opportunity to report the results is pretty easy to provide. Not everyone in a large introductory class will have an opportunity to present, but a single class period should allow for at least four different individuals or "teams" to review whatever they've been up to. Inevitably when I have papers due in a large introductory course, I ask people to read them. Years ago, five or six students would march to the front of the room, take the podium, and read, just like in a poetry class. In recent semesters, it's been like pulling teeth to get even one such volunteer. The last time I tried this little "symposium" trick in freshman biology, I asked them to write on their papers: *I am not afraid to read this paper in front of the class.* Then I asked for volunteers. After about five minutes of silence, a senior business major in a 100-level biology class came to the microphone and did an excellent job.

Then I asked for questions; in my view, students owe a fellow student presenter some kind of a response. More silence. So I asked them to write three questions on the back of their papers, questions they were afraid to ask. Out of 200+ papers collected that morning, 70 percent indicated they were not afraid to do the reading, and all had three questions on the back. Seventy percent were not afraid, they said, but only one individual would actually do it. All had questions, but none would ask. Something was going on here that made it very difficult to bring this particular instructional technique—the peer teaching that accompanies reading—to a large class. I am more than willing to concede that whatever I was doing in that lecture section that semester threw a real fear into my students, a true fear of standing up and sharing their unique version of the shared experience of writing a paper based on a natural history museum visit. I assume that "something" is my age, and that in a course taught by someone younger and more glamorous, there would again be a parade to the podium. I'm not willing to admit that "something" might be a wholesale cultural shift to submissiveness and unwillingness to assume a leadership position in light of early third millennium current events. And all we're talking about here is a truly harmless act of mild intellectual leadership.

One feature of the field program that is difficult to reproduce on city campus is student awareness of one another's efforts at research. In other words, when you see everyone else struggling constantly, having both success and failure, and talk about the experience all the time informally, then you come to have respect for the very act of original investigation. This shared experience is not a feature of typical university coursework. Back on campus, most students study by themselves, often in a corner of the library with headphones on, or in their apartments, sometimes in small groups. And most of what's being studied is someone else's original work, whereas in the field, everyone watches everyone else work and the students themselves generate most of what's being studied. This difference between "study" in the two settings is a fundamental and qualitative one. Granted, it's easy to do research on city campus, but undergraduates who do such research usually end up sharing their daily experience with a professor and a couple of graduate students, all of whom know full well that they're generating knowledge in addition to acquiring it. Incorporating this shared day-to-day struggle with original investigation into a large introductory science course, however, is another found problem in teaching.

The success of any session-ending symposium depends on mutual understanding of the labor involved in, and implied by, the presentations. A shared sense of what it takes to bring a project to closure builds respect for one another's efforts. This sense is a distinct feature of professional scholarship and intellectual labor regardless of the discipline. Artists and musicians know full well what it takes to produce art and music. Few, if any science students, especially those in the introductory courses, know from original experience what it takes to produce scientific discoveries, such as a single arrow on a metabolic diagram. In my opinion, this difference between art and music on the one hand, and science on the other, also is a rather large found pedagogical problem. The teacher who solves this problem, especially through course design, and very much especially at the secondary and university levels, will have made a major contribution to the lives of teachers and students everywhere.

Reflecting on the opportunities and constraints provided by the ideal learning environment of western Nebraska, and on the teaching lessons we got as a result of evading the constraints and seizing the opportunities, it seems like those lessons are not only fundamental and obvious, but also forgotten ones in much of higher education. I have no broad and carefully designed national survey to back up my impressions, only thirty-six years of classroom experience, thirty-six years of listening to what my colleagues from across the country were doing, thirty-six years of service on faculty committees dealing with coursework and curriculum. I have yet to hear anyone invoke the principle of course design known as *making your students do what I do in order to be and stay a professional* ———. Instead, I hear a whole lot of discussion of *what students should know*, and I see a whole lot of behavior leading to an image of teacher + textbook as authority rather than fellow explorer.

I honestly believe that this authority figure plus passive audience model, especially in the large enrollment courses at our major universities, is not healthy for either our nation or the institution of personal freedom. When average Americans are hit with up to 30,000 commercial messages a day, plus an additional ~200 personalized phone calls, E-mails, FAXes, and the like, then a college professor showing PowerPoint slides of the photosynthesis reactions to 230 business, English, and exercise science majors just doesn't work (Balzar, 2002). If there is anything at Cedar Point truly worth exporting back to the city, it's this model of learning by being, a model that may touch the deep roots of human evolutionary origins. When instead of just *learning* what someone else had to say about hunting, gathering, making clothes, and raising babies so we could go be lawyers and marketing specialists, we all had to *be* hunters, gatherers, clothesmakers, and child-care providers so we could see daylight tomorrow morning. I'm not suggesting we should go back to the caves, literally, only metaphorically, if we're trying to teach someone something, no matter what our discipline or specialty.

5

THE DESIGN OF A
WRITING ASSIGNMENT

The words we write for ourselves are always so much better than the
words that we write for others.
—Sean Connery (as William Forrester, in *Finding Forrester*)

How do you give a student a writing assignment that he or she cannot fulfill by downloading something off the Web? How do you give
a writing assignment that teaches something you want to teach, especially the transferable skills that are such an essential part of any
good university education, yet requires a student to reach beyond his
or her perceptions of the world in a meaningful way? These questions, which are probably the same question just phrased differently,
are some of the central pedagogical ones in higher education today,
and probably in middle and secondary schools as well. I don't claim
to have succeeded in answering them, but I know for a fact that I've
come close with paper assignments in various courses, assignments
that are a direct extension of the Cedar Point experience. In other
words, I saw something happening in the field course, and knew I
had to make that same something happen back on city campus.
Every student had to generate a product that was both unique and at
the same time useless from a practical point of view—for example—a
piece of art disguised as science. The goal, of course, was to teach the
art, rather than the technology, of science, to inspire originality instead of always worrying about the execution.

The one criterion for these works is probably educational blas-
phemy: If a student actually does the assignment, then he or she gets
full credit. I never grade students on how well they do such an assignment; I always grade them on whether they actually did what was
requested, which is usually to generate three full typewritten pages
on some subject. The subject is routinely one about which you could

easily generate a short paragraph, such as why such-and-such plant is your personal favorite of all the ones on campus. Obviously the subject itself is a key element of such papers, as is the restriction that students may not mention their own families, money, politics, agriculture, medicine, the military, sex, sports, or religion. Students usually and predictably produce the first two sentences quickly and easily. It's the next three pages that are the education. That is why I give full credit for a successful attempt.

Before elaborating on the strategy behind some of my more outrageous writing assignments, I'd like to comment briefly on pencil and paper—the two cheapest and most basic elements of the educational enterprise. P&P also are, or at least can be, among the most powerful of a teacher's tools. This rather fundamental principle of education often seems to be lost on some of my fellow faculty members, and increasingly so in a multimedia age. I have asked many of my colleagues the simple question: What's in your students' notebooks following a multimedia, showpiece, lecture? If they have bothered to look, their answers are about the same as mine, namely, "not much." One faculty member, a winner of my university's highest award for teaching, admits to "going back to the overhead," as a substitute for the blackboard. The choice between the two was made only because the writing is magnified enough on the screen so that students can see it from the back of a 230-seat auditorium. So he writes on the overhead as he explains physiology, conjuring up images of my left-handed organic chemistry teacher, in the early 1960s, who would start at the left side of a blackboard that reached all the way across the front of a large lecture hall, holding an eraser two feet long. This professor wrote equations and formulas as he talked, filling the board with one hand and erasing with the other. When he got to the end of the board, he walked back and started over. He did all this at a *human* pace. Needless to say, my chemistry notebook was pretty full. My colleague teaches in an auditorium equipped not only with an overhead projector, but also with two computers (Mac and PC; with PowerPoint, of course), Web access, video projector, a video presenter (document camera), a VCR, videodisc player, tape deck, 2 × 2 slide projector, 16-mm movie projector, podium- and portable microphones. He's ditched everything but the overhead, plus his portable microphone. Why? Because there is something in his students' note-books afterward.

Pencil and paper return our business to the human pace. Except for golf tournaments and baseball games, television—upon which our children feed several hours a day and that, some pundits claim, is altering our mental state accordingly—rarely proceeds at a human pace. If it did, we wouldn't watch it, mainly because we watch it to get away from whatever human pace experiences we've had during a typical day at the office. Unfortunately, there is some evidence that certain features of television stimulate one of our deepest instincts in a way that not only shortens our overall attention span, but also is outright addictive (Kubey and Csikszentmihalyi, 2001). MTV is the shining example of programming that aims directly at what Kubey and Csikszentmihalyi call our "orienting response." This instinct, which also turns a neonate's head toward the morning window light, is our response to a sudden stimulus. Music videos generate such stimuli continuously. But we're not required to take either notes or an exam on MTV, and aside from the few of us who eventually get into the rock video business, we don't even need to remember what we saw, heard, or felt. There's something almost primal about pencil and paper, however, or, for that matter, wet clay. This is why art is not a frill, but an essential component of education even for a nascent scientist.

Art is constant practice at reaching into our most elementary resources—our ideas and perceptions that are the essence of our humanity—and recording these resources using some simple means. Humans interact with one another across vast stretches of time and space by recording their experiences, permanently, with their own hands, in a medium that does not degrade easily. We don't have to do our art well; we just have to do it continuously, in order for it to be-come a transferable skill. Writing functions equally as well, although it's much easier for a student to subvert a writing assignment than it is to fake a drawing. Art teachers typically watch their students pro-duce drawings; biology teachers assign a paper from the front of a big auditorium, then walk out of class, leaving behind people with easy access to the Web, or to a library, which fewer and fewer of them are learning to appreciate. Thus when a biology teacher assigns a paper, he or she must also subvert the process, preempting the students' power to do the same thing.

Obviously the only way to accomplish this feat is to make a paper assignment that can't be faked, or at least for which the fakery is relatively obvious. I don't claim to have achieved this goal completely, but I do claim to have made the contest between student and faculty a more even one. More important, I know for a fact that out of any class, at least a few students will thrive on these strange writing assignments and a few will generate brilliantly original works. I also know that this originality will simply leap out at me from the page. So how is this contest with the media to be played? I suspect there are many answers, but here is mine: *Get rid of the media.* This goal is behind my policy of not accepting a paper that mentions family, money, health, agriculture, the military, politics, sex, sports, or religion. This condition is written into my syllabus. Family, money, health, agriculture, the military, politics, sex, sports, and religion *are* the subjects of the media; indeed they may be synonymous with "the media." So I simply eliminate them as legitimate topics for discussion. What's left? Plenty. Thousands of pages, literally thousands, indeed tens of thousands, over the past thirty-six years, that my students have filled with legitimate material having nothing whatsoever to do with those forbidden topics.

These two aspects of my writing assignments, namely, the list of forbidden topics and the individualized subject, no matter how many students are in class, are a direct result of the Cedar Point Field Parasitology experience. Family, money, health, agriculture, the military, politics, sex, sports, and religion are rarely mentioned late at night when we play go-around-the-room, or sit outside the CPBS gate watching stars. But the fact of this list is also a product of sunrises and sunsets—e.g., aspects of nature that are completely beyond the control of humanity. Biologists who work in the field learn very quickly that many events in nature cannot be controlled, and over the years we come to believe that this particular characteristic of our planet is a rather fundamental one. Having come to that conclusion, we inevitably become aware of how naive some of our politicians and businessmen can be, especially regarding natural systems. Prior to the development of atmospheric science, we probably watched a beautiful sunset and called it an act of God, thus supernatural. No man could ever produce one on call for his bride to be. We now know what abiotic factors conspire to produce beautiful sunsets, but that knowledge gives us no more power than the aborigines had over their production. Or, as Laura Duclos, one of my Cedar Point students so aptly put it, "The child will wait for the rainbow, but the rainbow will not wait for the child." So my intent with writing assignments is to draw students away from that list of subjects over which they probably have some control, and lead them closer to a real experience with the planet. I know it takes a leap of faith to believe that a list of forbidden topics can turn this trick, but if you are a teacher, just try it.

The other element of this exercise in media avoidance, however, is the assignment itself, which I try to make a highly individual one. For example, one of the most effective teaching devices, and one that I use about every three or four years, is: Pick a single plant, growing somewhere on campus, and write three pages of double-spaced typing, telling me why you chose that plant. The only condition is that this plant must be a perennial, knee-high or higher; and, of course, the paper based on a student's interactions with this plant cannot mention the media subjects. There are far more such plants on campus than there are students in any class. I suggest they pick some plant that they pass by every day; although they think this suggestion is helpful, it's actually subterfuge. Knowing they must write four papers on it, they begin studying it every time they walk past, something they would never do if not encouraged by a point-generating option. A typical first assignment is some permutation of the question: Why did you pick this particular plant? A little bit of imagination produced numerous versions of the same question: Why did you *not* pick three others? What function did you expect this plant to perform for you personally that the others could not? You get the picture. As for the papers themselves, it's well to remember their fundamental property, namely, that the first two sentences are easy ones to write whereas the remaining three pages are the education. After a few years of reading such papers, you become well acquainted with a few of our university's more prominent trees.

Sometimes the landscape architects' work erodes the individualistic qualities of such an assignment. What is the favorite student plant, statistically speaking, on this campus? A staghorn sumac planted at the west end of a building named Andrews Hall is probably the most popular plant on campus, although the actual number of papers about it is fairly small, considering the number that have been written. Why this particular sumac? First, it is a very dramatic plant; I also notice it almost every day, and I make it a point to walk past it, taking one sidewalk choice over another, in order to see it up close, especially in the summer and early fall. Second, Andrews Hall is an archtypical liberal arts edifice in which all the English courses are taught. Students usually exit this west door in order to get to psychology or math classes in two other buildings, which between them house most of the arts and sciences faculty and their classrooms, walking past (or through!) a large Richard Serra sculpture in the process. So, on any given weekday, a large fraction of the university's student traffic passes through these three buildings, past the staghorn sumac, and past Serra's *Greenpoint*.

My writing assignments, at least those semesters when I've asked for favorite plants, confirm what every landscape architect knows well: put a dramatic plant somewhere near traffic and not only will people notice it, they also will actually think about it once in a while. The same principle applies to gigantic, curved, sheets of inch-thick steel set at angles into the concrete: *Greenpoint*. Besides, the students have about as much control over the sumac as they have over a rainbow, or over the impact Serra's dramatic work of art has on the surrounding buildings. But to be fair to the other thousands of plants on campus, very many other than that particular sumac have been chosen. One student was so taken with a marijuana plant growing between the railroad tracks near campus that I allowed it to be her subject for the semester. Fortunately for her, nobody smoked it for nearly four months.

And what are other typical paper assignments to be written on the same individual plant selected by a student? They vary, but in one particularly successful semester they were: (paper 2) choose a single leaf and explain the role that leaf plays in the plant community surrounding your chosen individual plant; (paper 3) describe the interactions your plant has with human beings other than yourself; and (paper 4) describe the changes that have occurred in your plant during the semester. To write paper 4, they need to be warned that something like this assignment is forthcoming, so that they make some observations, although the act of writing the first three automatically produces many of the needed observations.

Keeping in mind that the students given such an assignment are in introductory biology, we might ask how they perform. Some, of course, choose not to do this assignment at all, or any writing assignment for that matter, or even to come to class regularly. Some produce truly brilliant, creative, and insightful compositions; this kind of writing is a true pleasure to read. A few begin with a sentence something like "I chose the big oak tree behind Hamilton Hall because it reminds me of a tree on my grandfather's farm . . ." then proceed to tell me, in three typewritten pages, about their grandfather's farm. Needless to say, they have to write this paper over again. (Remember: Family is among my forbidden topics.) But the vast majority of students truly do try to actually study a single plant for a semester. I envision them returning as financially successful alumni two decades hence, seeing their chosen plant, and experiencing an emotional shock that reaches all the way to their checkbooks.

How do I grade these papers? There are only two categories: (1) did, or (2) didn't do, the assignment. If the student does the assignment, he/she gets full credit; if not, he/she gets to do it over again, and over, and over, until it's actually done. That is, the "do-overs" continue until I actually get three typed double-spaced pages, one-inch margins, telling me for the full three pages why they picked this particular individual plant, without once mentioning family, money, health, agriculture, the military, politics, sex, sports, or religion. I circle things that a student would normally be marked off for in other classes (e.g., misspelled words, incomplete sentences, etc.), and I use brackets and stars to highlight good ideas, original thoughts, particularly insightful observations. As for the feedback, instead of getting told what they did wrong, they get told how to make better grades in other classes. That is, I use their mistakes as a means of giving them advice on what not to do in papers for other courses. What do *I* learn from reading and marking these papers? I learn what every teacher knows well, but few elected school-board members, senior administrators, and trustees know (or want to admit) at all—namely—every student is different. Furthermore, as a group, they are extremely varied. Increasingly we treat them, however, as a homogeneous body of customers. This treatment, a product of "management" and "administration," is a another fundamental flaw in our system.

In the General Zoology course, which I taught for many years before my biological sciences department decided to no longer allow it to count for majors' credit, I often handed out a different mollusc shell to each student. In one diabolically inspired assignment I asked for the three typewritten pages on why their shell was better than the one that their lab partner got. In another, I asked for five different piece of jewelry to be designed from that one shell, and a statement about what statement the student was making when he or she wore that particular piece of shell jewelry. Obviously I had to relax the constraints a little bit on this one, but not much. The jewelry assignment produced one of the most stunning student papers, and indeed one of the most wonderfully original and even borderline inspirational pieces that I have ever read. What made it inspirational? The sheer joy, rebellious originality, rather extraordinary use of the material, and drive. The writer was also a scholarship athlete on a national championship team. How many papers have I read? The best estimate is about 30,000, which translates into about 90,000 pages of double-spaced student writing. When a student produces one that sticks in your memory for years, one that you cannot forget, then you have been given a teacher's ultimate reward. Here is that paper, written by Billie Jean (Winsett) Fletcher, and included here with her permission:

Who Gives a Shell

Billie Jean Winsett

After receiving an "A" in Dr. John Janovy's zoology course at the University of Nebraska, I decided to spend the summer in my hometown of Boonville, Indiana. Although I was once molded into its conservative atmosphere, Dr. Janovy's course and the rest of the college scene reshaped me into a bold, unique personality. Thus I challenged the tradition that summer and demonstrated my new knowledge and appreciation for the animal kingdom. I wore my shell jewelry.

I bounced off the plane on Monday to meet my parents. Immediately their eyes became wide with disgust. Although they blushed with shame as they claimed me as their daughter, I did not feel embarrassed, because Dr. Janovy marveled at the beauty and wonder of unique characteristics. I was beautiful, I was wonderful, for I was unique. I had an exquisite nose ring—a shell nose ring. The nose ring silently rested on the side of my left nostril. It was a beautiful nose ring—a spiraled, light-brown, two-centimeter shell. This piece of jewelry shouted my boldness, my continuing search for authenticity. A scientist is not revered for submitting preconceived principles. A person is not noticed while living within the boundaries of accepted ideas. I would not be confined.

On Tuesday my friends and I celebrated my birthday by dining at an expensive restaurant. Dresses, jackets, and flashy jewelry were flaunted. I also decided to flaunt my wealth, but not my monetary wealth. Rather, I chose to flaunt my wealth of knowledge. By studying zoology as a foreign language, I absorbed thousands of new vocabulary words. I no longer needed slang, breathless words that fill empty space. I had important scientific matters to discuss. Why were there so few scientists that study sponges? Why had Libbie Henrietta Hyman not been equaled and replaced? Why did page 22 of the zoology lab book indicate that fibers of the *Hydra* nerve net might not be detected under the university's compound microscopes, when most educated people know that it would take a good electron microscope to see the structures? I wanted questions; I wanted discussion; I wanted answers. Meaningless conversation had no place in my educated life. I refused to be corralled by social fences. I would gallop in my own pasture. Thus, I accented my silk blouse with a green tie that had that little brown shell attached in the center as a tie pin. I would not be conservative.

On my third day home, I began to feel the friction that the resistance of old traditions against new realities were producing. It was Wednesday, the day when the beginning of the week mingles with the end of the week, causing anxiety and relief simultaneously. Wanting to be released from this tension, I turned to nature for counseling. I hurriedly put on my camouflage T-shirt and denim shorts. I flung off my shoes and placed a golden ring on my third toe. Mounted on the top of my gold ring was a sturdy brown shell that stretched from the bottom of my toe to its neighboring joint. I ran barefoot through the forest and to the edge of a stripper pit, for there is freedom in fleeing. The lake was dangerously deep but deeply delightful. As I walked, I referred to each animal by their name—their genus-species name, which I learned in zoology. Nature is a sanctuary of independent but accepted variations, behaviors, ideas. The toe ring reminded me that if I remained on top of those that want to trample me, I would not be broken, no matter how delicate I might appear. If I remained strong in my convictions, I would not be crushed. I would not be conquered.

After that walk with my palm in Mother Nature's hand, I realized the dramatic effect ecology had on the human race. Thus on Thursday, I decided to wear my life cycle necklace. This was a thin, black leather string that only completed its circle when the brown shell connected the two strings. The necklace was somewhat like a string tie, yet the shell would not move down, it would only move up toward the neck. Humans are in the center of the food chain and life cycle; it encircles us so that we may conveniently reach for any part of the circle. The animals of the world connect this circle and keep it continuous. Yes, as Dr. Janovy emphatically asked, What are we doing to the planet? With each ecological disaster the human race creates, the shell on the necklace rises an inch toward our neck. Just as the shell on the necklace cannot be moved down, and the effects of human mistakes cannot be erased. We humans will choke ourselves by choking the biological environment. We are cheating ourselves by choking ourselves, ignoring nature's rules of ecological symbiosis. Many argue that tomorrow will take care of itself. I will not be convinced.

On day five of my summer vacation, I attended a relative's wedding reception. The bride was dazzling, and the groom was darling. Yet the focus of the table where I was sitting was not on the newlyweds but on my sparkling ring. On my third finger was the shell mounted on a golden band and surrounded by gems of ruby, emerald, amethyst, and diamond. Like the knowledge and spirit I contained, my jewelry was intriguing. People gazed in wonderment, afraid to touch. The ring represented new ideas and styles in a way that demanded attention just as the rest of my shell jewelry. I would not be confined by tradition. I would not be conservative in order to relate to my peers. I would not be convinced that the environment is not the center of our dazzling world. I would not be conquered, for I would not break. In my unique ways, just as the shell jewelry, I will coruscate.

I suggest resisting the temptation to "correct" any of Ms. Fletcher's style or usage with which you may not agree. That temptation may be more difficult to resist when you read a second piece about this same shell that she produced after being sent to the Sheldon Memorial Art Gallery. But I've spent some time with these two papers, reading them over and over again. Once in a while, in my mind, I edit them. Then I back off and ask myself what it is that I have done. The answer is never very flattering, but always reinforces my belief that the teacher's job is to get something original out of a student, and the more original, the more unique, the more expressive, philosophical, and metaphorical, the better. Society as a whole will edit this student soon enough; but *Who Gives a Shell?* will never lose its power, nor will *The Light Not in the Horizon*, which you will get to read in Chapter 11. At the end of the semester, you only hope that you've given a piece of shell jewelry to all your students.

I now teach Biodiversity; to get a mental picture of this course, imagine General Zoology, Introductory Botany, Mycology, Protistology, Microbiology, Systematics, Biogeography, and Evolution all smashed into a single semester. Nevertheless, Biodiversity offers some writing assignment possibilities that the beginning courses do not because it is a majors' core course, and biology majors *ought* to know certain things regardless of the fact that most of them are premeds. Thus in this class a teacher can get by with things that would drive an undeclared nineteen-year-old freshman inclined toward elementary education straight up the wall. For example, in Chapter 3 I mentioned the trick of asking for an analysis of the original descriptions of five congeneric species and subsequent use of those descriptions as "text" for three additional papers. Various permutations of such assignments include picking a species that has been studied for a hundred years and finding five papers on it, at least one from the current year's literature, one from the year a student's parent was born, and one from the year a grandparent was born (see Chapter 6). As explained in the next chapter, in those paragraphs describing emergent properties of libraries, this particularly ornery task could be the most educational one of all. On the other hand, some version of this task is one of the easiest things to design, not only in biological sciences but also in any other subject area taught at a university.

Although I never anticipated writing a book about teaching, thus have not kept a record of everything my mostly freshman and sophomore students have done using their individual "collections" of specimens or descriptions, I did keep a few of the better papers. From that file, I know my students have done the following (some relaxation of the forbidden subject list is needed for a few of these assignments):

1. Written a critical commentary on the data sets required to actually do alpha taxonomy on the genus selected, addressing the problem of whether species descriptions are useful in phylogenetic studies of the selected taxon.

2. Explored the molecular diversity of the five species using isozymes, allozymes, RAPDs, and RFLPs (all molecular techniques), explained what they hoped to accomplish by doing this research, then put their work into a larger context (which they had to identify).

3. Pretended they were the university chancellor and had just signed a $1 million contract, paid for with taxpayer money, to install a forty-foot bronze sculpture of one of their species in the courtyard of a new honors dorm, then answered all the criticism (without mentioning the forbidden subjects).

4. Pretended they had discovered five new species of their genus and decided to name those species after people, thus explained why they honored those particular individuals with a specific epithet.

5. Designed natural history museum galleries to showcase one of their species.

6. Written screenplays using their species in roles that were intended to influence the way humans interacted with the natural world.

7. Written short stories about their species, stories intended to make some target audience choose biology as a career.

8. Analyzed the graphics in their descriptions, then compared the visual communication techniques with those used in various pieces of art in the Sheldon Memorial Art Gallery on our campus.

9. Written grant proposals, including budgets, for replacing the type specimens of their five species, and in the process analyzed the dangers they might face in the type localities today.
10. Done historical research on the careers of their descriptions' authors, trying to discover the directions their careers might have taken after or before they wrote those papers.
11. Described the biotic communities from which their species came.

This (partial) list suggests that a small collection of original species descriptions can be used as a metaphorical landscape, to be explored in any number, indeed an almost infinite number, of ways. Only a teacher's imagination and courage limit the length of such a list. This view of published research as landscape to be explored, even by freshman, is a direct result of the Field Parasitology course at Cedar Point Biological Station. The multiple views of a single course, as described in Chapter 3, are not unlike the multiple views of nature as presented by artists and writers. There is no less abstraction in a DNA gel showing the relationship between two species than there would be in a David Smith sculpture of that same relationship. There is no less alteration of reality in a single scientist's approach to an undomesticated system like the Nebraska Sandhills than there would be in a Monet painting of that scientist's study site. And a professional photographer, with a full set of lenses, could stand in the middle of the South Platte River, where my Cedar Point students have stood for nearly thirty years, and record images at least as diverse as that foregoing list of writing assignments. We have learned a very valuable, and exportable, Cedar Point lesson when we finally come to understand the full range of ways that human beings have recorded their interactions with their surroundings. What remains to be learned by most of my colleagues is the technique for incorporating this full range of visions into the tasks they require of their students. I sometimes wonder if what my colleagues actually need to do is acquire the artists' disdain for paradigm, the poet's reverence for individuality, and the photographer's set of mental lenses, before stepping into the science classroom.

6

A PREDICTABLE SUPPLY
OF MATERIAL

Take me, Lord, to an unexplored planet teeming with new life forms.
—E. O. Wilson (from *Naturalist*)

Each year I fill out a request for teaching supplies. Every teacher in the nation probably does this, and teachers throughout the world probably do the equivalent. What are these supplies? In my case they range from microscope slides, cover glasses, and petri dishes to living earthworms, rotifers, soil nematodes, to common grocery-store items such as mushrooms, to preserved snakes and turtles. The best thing that can be said for these items is that I don't have to make or collect them and most of the time they are delivered to my door at the university. The worst thing that can be said for them is that they are often unrepresentative of their respective phyla (e.g., earthworms), and that they arrive completely out of context—that is—missing the environment in which they live. Even biological supply houses occasionally fail to deliver on their catalog promises, however, so I do get back orders. By the time I find out the materials are not going to arrive, it's usually too late to write a new lab exercise. Although context is a problem regardless of the subject, teachers of literature, music, philosophy, mathematics, and chemistry are never faced with an unpredictable supply of material. But an inadequate and unpredictable supply of living materials is the bane of any biology teacher's existence.

In an ideal world such as we find at Cedar Point, there is never an inadequate supply of materials. Everything you need to do your job is immediately available, right at your fingertips, alive, and in its proper context. Back on city campus, very little of what you need is immediately available, even less of it is at your fingertips, not much of it is alive, and none of it is in the proper context. This difference was articulated most clearly by a high-performing honors student named Wendy Allen, who, near the end of our time at the field station, decided not to do my daily writing assignment (the question set), but instead to express her reactions to our first field trip:

> The first day of class, I was overwhelmed with information. I simply could not comprehend all that was going on during the day and all that had happened by the end of the day. I was quite upset by this fact, because I had never experienced something quite like that before. I felt as though I was the only lost soul standing knee-deep in Dunwoody Pond. However, after I got to know the other students, I realized that I was not the only one who felt that way the first day of class.
>
> Quite frankly, I was very angry the first day of class because it seemed as though I was getting rapid-fire information all day long. It took me quite a while to realize that you taught your class that way out of necessity. I did not realize how short a five-week session actually is for a class such as this one.

With her biologist's hat on, Wendy was actually talking about the difference between town and country—between extreme pedagogical poverty and equally extreme wealth, respectively, at least to a biologist. Indirectly, however, she was also talking about having been taught for twelve years in an impoverished setting, likely out of necessity. How do you solve this problem of trying to teach biology in a biological wasteland? How do you solve the problem of trying to teach *anything* in a relative wasteland? Well, first, you have to recognize that it *is* a problem. Second, you have to accept the fact that no matter what you do, you can never find a substitute for real stuff in proper context. What is "real stuff in proper context"? Snails in a pond a mile off the road, insects under a fallen log deep in the forest, invertebrates in a stretch of rocky intertidal shoreline, all qualify. I'm not quite sure what constitutes equivalent material in the arts and humanities, but if a student *makes* art and literature as an essential component of *studying* art and literature, then that's a first approximation. (See Brent Wilson's *The Quiet Evolution*, for a discussion of this teaching principle, called Discipline-Based Art Education.) You can't always find a substitute for real stuff in context, but you can make a brave attempt to do so, which is better than no attempt. In any case, even partial success will change the character of your teaching. That is a major take-home lesson from any field program. In the case of biology, building an Eden means a commitment to bring living organisms into the city classroom, and to bring at least some of their environment along with them.

The brave attempt to fulfill this commitment begins when you walk into a university building whose architectural style is best described as Lowest Bidder Utilitarian and whose walls reek of institutionalized conservatism. How might such an environment be turned into a metaphorical cattail marsh? You need to find something that works like real stuff, that has some of the same properties, regardless of whether or not it's alive in the literal sense. You can't write those specifications on the order form about to be stuck in the mail to Carolina Biological Supply Company or Sigma Chemical. Nobody keeps this kind of material in stock, at least on purpose, except for those who own several square miles of tallgrass prairies, eastern deciduous forest, rocky intertidal coastline, northwestern old-growth forests, or Sonoran Desert. So you have to make your own real stuff—or something that has a few of the same properties—out of whatever is at hand. I'm convinced that this task can be accomplished and that supply issues can sometimes be addressed with creativity and hard work. However, context is the most difficult part of real life to duplicate or replace.

As an illustration of the context problem, consider an art history course constructed from a slide set whose subjects span periods from the Cro-Magnon to the Post-Modern. A student in such a course could readily memorize images, names, museums where various pieces are now found, and perhaps even financial transaction records, depending on the particular items. A faculty member could conveniently ask for this kind of information to be returned on an examination, and such an exam would be easy to grade. In fact, you could probably put 300 people in an auditorium, offer them this kind of course, give multiple-choice tests using mark-sense forms, and tell the administration you were being efficient. Indeed, if you were an art department chairperson, you might have been forced into this kind of a teaching endeavor by the financial constraints of your institution. As an extreme departure from reality, this particular course might easily be offered on the World Wide Web as "distance learning." Then an institution might actually make some money by charging tuition and giving college credit for something anyone with a library card could do on his or her own for free.

But if you were the teacher in that course, you would inevitably have this nagging feeling that something was just not right. Your students would very likely not be reading about economic, social, and military history of the period in which art was made, they would never mix pigments, and never struggle with the logistics of obtaining a block of marble or the right brush. They would never endure the highs and lows of an artist producing original works, and would never get a sense of how much of the surrounding art—contemporary with the pieces they were studying—had been destroyed in the decades or centuries or wars since it was made. Nor would they learn much about the personal lives of the people who produced these works. Your students would never walk in a painter's shoes, never get caught up in religious controversies surrounding certain pieces, and never try to earn a living by making sculpture at a particular time and place in history. In other words, the context would be missing. Context is the main thing missing from information technology, and context cannot be supplied over the Internet. Sitting at your computer, you can get your words into the face of someone halfway around the world in an instant, but it might take a lifetime to understand that same person's worldview and you have no idea what his dinner smells like.

That last sentence might well provoke an instant objection from somebody wedded to distance learning, and who would contend, probably quite strongly, that you can supply *anything*, even context, via the Web. Indeed, some of my colleagues in biology get all or most of their classroom materials from the Web. However, the minute a student is handed an insect net or a bucket, pointed in the direction of the nearest pond and told to bring back a problem that could serve as his or her thesis work, then the context returns and the fallacy of our increasing dependence on information technology becomes obvious. There is a difference between natural materials and what comes across fiber optic cables, and unless your business is money, very little of the latter is real. The challenge, of course, is how to provide real stuff, regardless of the subject, in the information age. I submit that our first task is to understand that some information simply cannot be transmitted electronically and must be acquired by original experience. If that sentence sounds trite and obvious to you, then you are very likely an old-timer, if not in chronological age, then in spirit.

A field station functions for a biologist the same way that a major newspaper would function for a journalism teacher, could that newspaper be used as a combination classroom and laboratory. The only difference between the field station and the newspaper is that in the latter, you'd have to actually publish in order to complete the instruction (e.g., any high-school newspaper). Publication is not a must for students at Cedar Point. They can be real biologists "free," in the sense that nobody's tenure is at stake, no big grant must be obtained to impress their teacher, and there is no standard measure of success or failure, although there are standards for "done well" and "done in a shoddy manner." Even the teacher has total freedom in this respect. Field programs are one of the very few places where a teacher can very honestly say that the educational value received has little or no relationship whatsoever with success or failure as we commonly define the terms, that the learning is inherent in the doing.

Why is this the case—this break in the supposed link between educational value and success—and how might one export this characteristic back to city campus? These questions form the crux of our task. Educational value is routinely separated from "success," and many—if not most times—from content, too, when the task at hand requires behaviors that are broadly applicable to intellectual endeavor regardless of their nature. This simple rule is the underlying, although usually tacit, assumption upon which all laboratory exercises are based. The first step in building an Eden is to recognize the assumption for what it truly is, namely, the idealism that drives a teacher into his or her profession. The second step is to use the rule as a guiding principle of teaching, no matter what the situation. For example, here is an excerpt from a letter I routinely send to prospective graduate students who inquire about opportunities in our lab:

My mentoring goal is to produce a capable, self-confident, professional scientist instead of saving the world from parasites or winning a Nobel Prize. Thus my students write thesis proposals, are expected to interact with faculty members and other students in seminars, give papers at regional and national meetings. We try to choose problems that (1) are within our logistical and intellectual capabilities; (2) serve as serious teaching and learning devices; (3) can be done within a reasonable length of time; and (4) produce publishable results. Our program places a premium on human qualities—resourcefulness, willingness to communicate, ideas, patience with dumb animals, creativity, and insight—primarily because I honestly believe these are the qualities that transcend technological skills. The materials we work with also demand those qualities. The students who have been most successful here have been open-minded, self-confident, communicative, opportunistic, flexible, easy-going people without a lot of baggage; the other kinds have often been miserable.

The "materials we work with" are typically small fish—rarely larger than 6 cm—and beetles that are between 2 and 12 mm in length. We collect, culture, and dissect these organisms, studying the distribution of parasites in various organs. We also do experimental infections, using "spores" that are the size of red blood cells. These spores, in turn, develop from cysts that we handle with a three-hair brush the size of a pin. In order to do experimental infections, we must produce tiny uninfected animals, of a particular life cycle stage, and we must convince them to eat whatever we've decided to feed them. Although the small fish may respond as pets—coming to the top of a tank for their meals—the beetles are truly dumb and driven only, as far as I can tell, by their instincts. On the plus side, the insects thrive on flour, wheat germ, oatmeal, cornmeal, and a variety of other cheap cereal grain products straight from our local grocery store. With several species in culture, we have, in essence, a microscopic zoo. In my personal experience, there is nothing quite like a menagerie of truly wild animals or a garden full of truly wild plants, regardless of scale, to test—and *develop*—one's patience, resourcefulness, communication skills, insight and creativity—the transcendent qualities. In other words, we need real stuff.

Only creative and courageous teachers of science can regularly replace fake stuff with real stuff. Creativity helps one see materials in places where others cannot, or will not, recognize them. In other words, a creative person looks out into his or her backyard and sees a jungle. The courage is required to do something that your colleagues quickly recognize as relatively creative, especially when compared to their own efforts. Fortunately, for administrators, creativity and courage are easily maintained in a bureaucracy by a few simple words and phrases such as "thanks," "nice job," "that's a great idea," "good luck; let me know if you need some help." These phrases all work wonders and cost nothing; they are included in the "hundred right words" for people in leadership positions. Unfortunately, few academic administrators understand this simple principle of human-resource management. The good news is that creative and courageous teachers typically continue to behave in their characteristic ways regardless of what administrators say to or about them.

So how can biology teachers without ready access to a field site supply their students with real *living* stuff in context? What you need is something exceedingly cheap, very wild and alive, and available just about everywhere. The infusion culture probably comes as close to meeting these criteria as any other item. Unfortunately, infusion cultures come with two problems. First, you must have a microscope in order to use one and a strong—or nonfunctional—nose to sit with it through its early phases. Of course you can't really be a biology teacher without a microscope, or at least a hand lens, so let's assume you have a microscope. Flour beetles and seed packets let you teach biology at the hand lens level, but this material is a far step down the swampiness scale from an infusion culture. The second problem is a little more formidable, however, and that is the one of knowledge. You have to either know enough about the microorganisms that appear in this jar, or you have to be enough of a teacher to use exotic little creatures in your teaching without having a clue as to what these creatures are. Fortunately, this second problem—the teacher's ignorance—is easily avoided by having students describe these organisms and give them names. The oldest trick in the teacher's book: If you don't know what you're talking about, make the students generate the knowledge themselves.

What, exactly, is an infusion culture? It's a handful of dried vegetation in a jar with water. Within a few days, such a concoction grows an amazing diversity of microorganisms, including protozoa. An infusion culture is swamp in a jar. It stinks, *really* stinks. It defies easy description. It changes over the course of a few weeks, exhibiting a progression of life forms, some of which can be exceedingly active and dramatic. A teacher, however, must know enough about these life forms to use them skillfully, and this lack of knowledge on the part of teachers is a major problem in science education today. When university science curricula start with DNA and end with DNA, then the teaching enterprise is denied access to some of its most exciting, accessible, inexpensive, and captivating materials. Kids get excited about organisms, and people remain "kids" at heart until well into their college years. This latent childishness is the reason why the oldest trick in the teacher's book always works.

Biology teachers who understand this fundamental principle are always successful. In fact, biology teachers may well be kids who never grew up. This grown-up childishness is the main reason why we believe an infusion culture "swamp-in-a-jar" is so wonderful. Economics teachers act like grown-ups, mainly because they spend so much time and effort dealing with money and market forces, just like our parents. At my institution, economics teachers wear sport coats and ties and deal with business, but biology teachers wear jeans and deal with bugs and weeds. Biology teachers who deal only with DNA find themselves in about the same category as economics teachers—that is—spending their intellectual lives with things of practical value and monetary worth. An infusion culture clarifies these distinctions like no other predictable set of materials. For the price of a quart jar, a double handful of dried weeds, and water, you can predictably produce a literal, albeit microscopic, swamp.

What have we done with infusion cultures? The answer depends on the course. In an advanced protozoology lab, every student made his or her own culture, then traced its succession of protozoa for fifteen weeks, identifying and quantifying insofar as possible every species that appeared. We ended up with at least ten quite different communities of one-celled animals, each with its own characteristic faunal mix and population dynamics. Regardless of its outcome, the infusion culture part of the lab is always a hit. Personal possession, in this case of an individual project/stinky jar, strengthens a student's bond with the materials. The same principle applied regardless of the real stuff, from a single campus perennial plant to a single mollusc shell issued at the beginning of the semester. In all these cases, paper after paper must be written on the personal possession. Students in protozoology classes end up producing veritable theses, with real data sets and original illustrations. At the end, it's an emotional experience to dump your stuff into the garbage disposal, or, for that matter, to return your single mollusc shell with your last paper in order to receive credit. A certain kind of closure ensues.

In Biodiversity, we set up gallon-size infusion cultures at two-week intervals prior to the semester, so that several weeks later, in a single afternoon, students can reconstruct the succession in a roadside ditch. Because Biodiversity is a freshman-sophomore course, however, we can't spend fifteen weeks struggling with the techniques of protozoology. But the infusion culture can be appreciated by students of all ages. My father made me one when I was about ten, and then gave me his childhood toy microscope to study it. I was hooked immediately. Half a century later, I'm using this same material—swamp-in-a-jar—for several university classes. I was exceedingly fortunate in being able to take courses while a graduate student that enabled me to use materials such as infusion cultures effectively. These days are long gone at most large universities. If we have accomplished anything in the past quarter century, it's been to distance not only our young PhDs, but also our prospective K–12 teachers, from the enormous diversity of readily available raw materials in the life sciences. Specialization and molecular biology are the culprits. But as mentioned, asking students to develop their own knowledge from scratch lets a teacher duck the ignorance imposed by so-called modern biology. About all I've ever had to do to keep students working at developing their own knowledge from an infusion culture is say "great job!" about every ten minutes.

For a biology teacher, two items that come very close to approximating the infusion culture in terms of wildness and economy are commercial seed packets and stored products beetles of various kinds. Both are alive, and both can acquire a context fairly easily—life and context being the key elements necessary to teach real biology. Indeed, for either of these sources of material, contexts can be built by anyone from elementary school children to doctoral students to serious established researchers exploring conceptually important questions. The seed packets allow a teacher, and students, to avoid the "specialization and molecular biology" syndrome by being conveniently labeled; the seeds' scientific names can usually be found easily on the Web if they aren't on the packet. Thus all you have to be able to do is read and do a Web search to discover that the zinnias are *Zinnia elegans* and several species of *Tagetes* (marigolds) are available. (Yes, for common scientific names and airline reservations, the Web is useful!) The beetles are a different matter; identification can be a problem, but growing them usually is not. Agricultural researchers are able to find stored products beetles (e.g., meal worms and flour beetles) in about any location where people store commercial quantities of dry dog and cat food, flour, cornmeal, or cereal. Fortunately, you don't always have to insult your local grocer by asking for permission to search the back room. I've never had any problem getting beetles just by asking around. Our research stocks come from a USDA lab, but they get theirs from the surrounding community, especially the pet-food aisles.

The inquiry-based use of seed packets is an absolute no-brainer. Elementary and middle-school kids must do dozens of science-fair projects with seed packets annually. Any biology teacher ought to be able to quickly make a list of a hundred. I also know that students at any large university could do some of these same projects as honors theses, obviously on a larger scale and with more sophisticated design and conceptual underpinnings. In a given time, crowded plants don't grow as large as plants that are not crowded. That is a simple hypothesis that can be tested by kindergartners. That simple hypothesis quickly becomes a set of sophisticated yearlong class experiments when we list its many permutations and elaborations:

1. All species respond to crowding in similar ways.
2. Soil pH, porosity, etc. influence the crowding effect.
3. Mixed species assemblages do not exhibit crowding effects.
4. Some plant species can recover from crowding but others cannot.

This list of testable hypotheses could go on and on; the only limit to the number of hypotheses that can be written is the imagination of students and teachers. The increased sophistication comes from the added sources of variation, the added potential for interaction between parts. Depending on the part of the country and local school clientele, the seeds could come from a variety of sources, many totally free. Dirt is usually free, too. The only problem with plants is that they are not warm and fuzzy and they don't have large dark eyes. That is, plants don't remind us of ourselves. Plants don't run around and yelp or nestle in our arms like rabbits. But like rabbits, plants do die, and such death can serve a serious purpose in the classroom (see Chapter 10). Thus a teacher needs the right words and the right body language to truly engage students in an exercise involving plants.

The right words and the right body language are absolutely free for teachers as well as administrators, but there are often strong personal constraints on using these free, universally available, and pedagogically powerful resources. Teachers don't always see themselves as actors needing to become characters to capture someone's imagination, but teachers are, in many ways, actors whether or not they see themselves in that way. Thus inspiring young humans to love plants is a found problem in the teaching of biology. Inspiring young people to love rocks is a found problem in the teaching of earth science. Inspiring young people to love paintings, sculpture, and literature is a found problem in the teaching of humanities. The solutions to these found problems always involve, at least in part, acting. You have to *do* something to make other humans *love* something. Grown-ups with houses and windows usually don't have much trouble acquiring a love for plants, stones, and artwork, but by that time these humans are way past the student stage in life, at least officially. Maybe grown-ups with houses and windows, and their love of plants and paintings, are untapped free resources for teachers. I think these people are called parents and grandparents.

Why is all this discussion of acting and loving your stuff necessary in a book about idealism in education when every adult knows everything I've just written? The answer to that question is fairly straightforward: Idealism is the first casualty of practicality, even though idealism is the life's blood of our profession. Our goal, if we are biologists, is to put living organisms in the hands of our students, and to establish a realistic context around those organisms—that is—to

lead our students back to nature at some scale. This goal derives from
a fundamental characteristic of our discipline. We study an emergent
property—namely—life that emerges from a particularly organized
collection of water, carbon, nitrogen, hydrogen, oxygen, sulfur, and
the like. We know that we're missing the point if all we study is
carbon, nitrogen, hydrogen, and their interactions. By extension it is
legitimate to ask whether art and literature are also emergent properties, arising out of a particularly organized collection of ideas, long-
ings, mysterious inner drives, landscapes, and so forth. I honestly
believe the answer to this last question is "yes" (see Berlinski, 2002).
This discussion of what we, as adults, know, is necessary because we
adults so easily forget what we know, or lose faith that our knowledge
is of use to others. When we assess our own knowledge and experience as resources, we discover immediately that a rich supply of instructional material is usually right at our fingertips, staring us in the
face. I do understand that some schools cannot afford seed packets.
But I also understand that birds and squirrels find enough seeds in
the city parks to sustain themselves, and I fervently believe that
teachers are as resourceful as birds and squirrels.

The key to conversion of everyday materials into sources of wonder rests, in my opinion, on our ability to elevate our teaching and
learning to a plane above the subject matter itself. This idea is explored at some length in two other places (Chapters 3 and 8), but I
deal with it here again because I believe we need a constant reminder
of what is to be accomplished by the study of emergent properties.
For a college professor, the question of how phenomena emerge from
organization is certainly a legitimate one; at the university level we're
supposed to be at least somewhat philosophical, to strive for "added
value" in our teaching endeavors. Is there a place for the study of
emergent properties in elementary, middle-school, and high-school
classes? I firmly believe the answer to this question is a resounding
"yes!" Science is so often relegated to the servant's role, namely that
of providing humans with power over their environment. Yet science
is also a way of knowing (Moore, 1993). Our job as teachers of science is to produce people who, in the words of Lawrence Slobodkin,
"see the world with the intellectual equipment of a grown-up and the
innocence of a two-year-old . . ." Slobodkin (1992) further warns

that this goal is not easy to achieve. On one level, the question of what's happening in a pot to produce that little pumpkin seedling is a simple tool to focus our attention on the fact that extreme complexity can look deceptively simple. Put in the seed, add some water, and you get a plant. On another level, the question of what that particular seed is giving me today that I can use twenty years from now is a found problem in the study of emergent properties. Both of these levels are accessible by human beings from childhood to old age, although admittedly for a person in his or her nineties, perhaps the twenty-year period probably should be shortened!

Libraries, antique malls, museums, large areas of landscaping, supermarkets, and the yellow pages of any large city's phone book all possess emergent properties. They all contain meta-information, or an intangible entity that exists because the underlying collection of items has a certain set of properties. All such collections are the equivalent of metaphorical swamps, and can be used in about the same way as any natural area. What students learn from using these collections is a set of transferable skills. They learn how to learn. This kind of education could probably be called *metalearning*. The teacher's immediate goal is to convert a limited supply of unpredictable and inadequate teaching materials, lacking context, into an unlimited supply of predictable and adequate teaching materials embedded in an informative context. The long-term goal is to teach our students how to carry out this transformation—that is—how to turn fodder into gold. My presumption is that if a student acquires the transferable skills, then these skills can be applied to a large variety of problems, including those involving truly wild animals living out short ornery lives in dirty out-of-the-way places.

How do you convert something as commonplace as a supermarket into something as uncommon as a swamp? The answer is: Treat it as a place to be explored but deny your students the easy questions for which there are readily available answers. Swamps are notorious for their disorganized diversity, their long-term stability coupled with short-term change, and the difficulty of identifying their component parts. Supermarkets are equally notorious for their highly organized diversity, their mechanisms for immediately incorporating change into existing structure, and the ease of identifying their component parts. Therefore, all you have to do is figure out something that is in a supermarket but is not one of its component parts, so is thus immune to, or at least independent of, the organizing mechanisms. In other words, you turn the store into a swamp. You give the kid the metaphorical equivalent of an aquatic dip net and ask that he or she go find something that you know is there on the shelves, but is hidden in a certain way. I'm not truly convinced that "hidden" is an easy term to define in this case. Let's just say that "hidden" refers to something that is present, but that you don't know it's present unless you use this swamp in a particular manner. If we do our teaching correctly, then the student will come away from this encounter with a common institution knowing a "particular manner" of searching: He or she will have learned a little of how to learn.

Any chapter entitled A Predictable Supply of Material should probably end with a reference to the Wilson epigraph that opened this chapter (p. 73). There are many times when—strange as it seems—good old beat-up Earth appears to be that "unexplored planet teeming with new life forms." Although those "new life forms" are not literal ones, as in new species of butterflies and monkeys, it is clearly evident to any channel-flipping student of popular culture and cable news that we humans are populating this planet with the equivalent of new species. These sometimes seemingly alien invaders include innovations, inventions, tools formerly found only in pulp sci-fi magazines but now on the bench in every molecular lab, ideas spawned by all this technology, modern and post-modern art, rap music, the list is almost endless. Only die-hard literalists deny the obvious analogy between these purely cultural phenomena that so readily reproduce, evolve, and undergo adaptive radiation (Cavalli-Sforza and Feldman, 1981; Hofstadter, 1985). We are indeed populating our world with new life forms that in some ways redefine the term "life," not only for humans, but also for our fellow travelers on this only-known occupied planet. Surely in such a world there is a predictable supply of material readily available for every teacher. But just as surely, for a teacher of science, use of that supply has all the potential for separating us from the dirt, weeds, water, and rocks from which it all ultimately springs.

7

Questions

What does it mean when there is no food in the country and no food in the town?
—from a purported list of questions "put to candidates for Communist Party membership . . ." (Arthur Koestler, *The Invisible Writing*)

If my experience with undergraduates is any indication of what goes on in our K–12 enterprise, then outside of art classes, few students in America's public schools ever get asked what they would like to study. Instead, they are told what to study, or at least provided a narrow range of options. Fewer still are ever asked to find a question; virtually all are given questions then instructed to find answers. In other words, they are being trained to become problem-solvers, not problem-seekers. This distinction was pointed out to me, and to about 200 others, by a man named Richard McCommons, representing the American Institute of Architecture, who was delivering an exit interview to my university's College of Architecture after a reaccreditation visit. The question he addressed was: What must we do to become more influential, or to acquire a higher reputation at the national level? McCommons focused on the senior project, a skyscraper.

"We know how to design skyscrapers," he said, "that's a found problem for which we seek solutions. The problem is how to cram lots of people and offices into a relatively small area of earth. The solution is to build a very tall building. But to take the next step up, you need to find problems. That is, you need to become problem-seekers, not problem-solvers." Immediately after that meeting, I typed McCommon's words and taped them up in the lab.

McCommons' advice is related to the comment one often hears in academic circles, especially in the sciences, that so-and-so "asks good questions." By such flattery we mean that the answer to whatever problem so-and-so is posing, if eventually found, would be a conceptual contribution to the discipline. Is there an infinite supply of questions, including good ones? So it seems. The most influential scientific journals are very much still in business, Nobel Prizes are still being awarded, as are large grants from the National Science Foundation and the National Institutes of Health, and the biotech industry is thriving. Evidently, not only is someone asking good questions, but someone is also being relatively successful at finding good answers. In biology, however, there is a very close relationship between the questions that are asked and the systems used to answer them. A "system" consists of the particular organisms involved, the circumstances of their involvement, and our methods of study. This link between questions and systems is not necessarily a happy or productive one. It is much easier to find a good question than it is to find a good system with which to answer it; and, even when good systems are found, the answers they provide may not be general ones, but only specific to the particular set of organisms used. So the "asks good questions" characteristic could also be expanded into "not only asks good questions, but also finds good systems with which to address these questions."

Are good question-askers born that way, or can a teacher produce them? That is a good question! The terms "creative" and "rebellious" are often used in association, so there could easily be a genetic component to scientific talent, especially that exemplified by the more resourceful and imaginative researchers. On the other hand, because our entire educational system seems designed to produce problem-solvers instead of problem-seekers, perhaps we've managed to hide a lot of creative talent simply by not asking it to step forward, depending, instead, on those naturally inclined to challenge our prevailing paradigms. Thus the purposeful production of good, or even habitual, questioners is a found problem in science teaching.

How do we develop insight in a population of young people, especially when a significant fraction of this population has been told to shut up and do its homework for many years? There may be many techniques for accomplishing this task, but one day I decided that asking students to give me questions instead of answers might work. The results over the past several years may be worthy of discussion, but in my opinion, asking for questions instead of answers was perhaps one of the most valuable ideas that's ever come to me out of the blue. And the idea did come straight out of nowhere, although it may have happened when I was making out an exam, or grading one, and thinking: What a pain in the neck; exams are easier to take than to give. More likely, however, the question-set was a product of something that happened at Cedar Point, probably a result of discussion in class after a long day in the field. Routinely we finish a long and productive day with "go around the room," in which each student reflects on what we've accomplished, or not, and what we might do differently the next time. Maybe we went around the room one evening with each student contributing his or her best research idea, based on that day's fieldwork. After all, research ideas are nothing more than found problems. Or maybe it just dawned on me one early morning that McCommons' "problems" were really questions and that his faith—namely—that a person could be transformed from solver into seeker, was well founded.

Whatever its origin, the question set turned out to be an easily exportable aspect of the field parasitology course. At Cedar Point, the assignment gets modified periodically. Some years I ask for ten questions every class day, and at other times I ask for five, combined with an elaboration on the specific null hypotheses derived from those questions, and, of course, the systems one might choose to test these hypotheses. How do I "grade" such papers? I ask myself: If a student seriously tried to answer this question, especially through use of some amenable system, would he or she end up with enough data, and enough of a conceptual contribution, to write a publishable scientific paper, a masters thesis, or a doctoral dissertation? If the answer is "yes," the student gets a check mark by that question. Does everyone "ask good questions" with practice? No. Does everyone improve with practice? Not necessarily, but then not everyone practices seriously. What is the average grade on a daily question-set? About five or six out of ten—that is—about 50–60 percent.

In Field Parasitology, where most of my students are usually premeds, including many high performers back on city campus, there is usually a great deal of shock when I assure them that 60 percent on a question set is an excellent grade. These are students who by and large have never made 60 percent on anything. But in the real world of creative intellectual endeavor, 60 percent is truly an excellent grade. Any artist or fiction writer who sells 60 percent of his or her work becomes famous and earns a living, and if this sell rate continues for a lifetime, probably becomes rich. Any practicing scientist who ends up actually doing research on and publishing the results of 60 percent of his or her "good ideas," becomes a very successful scientist indeed. Baseball teams who win 60 percent of their games make the playoffs. Doctors who cure only 60 percent of their patients are in trouble, of course, but there are some statistics that demonstrate many problems for which doctors are consulted would eventually cure spontaneously anyway. Illness is not a problem that doctors seek; it's a problem that walks in their door. But artists, writers, truly creative scientists, and (evidently) influential architects, seek problems—typically within their own experiences—and if they solve 60 percent of the ones they find, they are doing pretty well. In my personal opinion, any teacher, anywhere, could easily devise some taste of the real world of creative endeavor for his or her students, using almost any set of material, simply by following McCommons' advice. So one day I just decided that back home on city campus I would become that "any teacher anywhere."

During a typical summer, a student in Field Parasitology generates nearly 100 questions in order to satisfy the daily written assignment portion of the course. Are 100 questions enough to set a particular student on a lifetime track of seeking problems instead of solutions? I don't know the answer, but I do know that the question-set idea was highly mobile and transferable. Thus when it became time to design laboratories for the Biodiversity course on city campus, the weekly question set was a no-brainer. The grading-policy section of their lab manual reads:

> **Questions:** There is a weekly written assignment consisting of a set of 10 questions, based on the previous week's lab exercise. You will automatically receive 7 points per question set if you turn them in on time; your lab instructor has the option of adding the other three points based on the insightfulness, seriousness, and depth of experience revealed by

the questions. These question-sets must be typed (word processor with dark ink is okay). The question-sets are worth 15 percent of your lab grade.

Taken out of context, this particular paragraph might meet with some derision from my fellow faculty members. Should a student receive 70 percent of the credit just for doing an assignment, just for turning in a page of ten questions? Yes. The vast and overwhelming majority of them have never, ever in their educational experience, been asked to generate ten questions, much less ten questions a week for fourteen weeks. Each question is worth only 0.1 percent of their lab grade, or 0.075 percent of their overall letter grade in Biodiversity, so I'm not giving away much of anything except an opportunity to try something different, and try it seriously. The "something different" in this case is the essence of original work, namely the seeking of problems rather than solutions.

What kinds of questions do students produce? Because I'm far more interested in a student's honest and serious attempts than in my own subjective judgment of "quality," the answer might seem a little tolerant of mediocre performance. But it's well to keep a couple of things in mind: first, the criterion of a publishable paper (see p. 89), and second, the element of creativity—perhaps "serendipity awareness" is a better term—in science. Even a cursory examination of the scientific journals reveals an enormous range of subject matter, approaches, and levels of success, all mostly dependent on a combination of appropriate technology and the particular system chosen for study. So the requirement that a question, if answered, leads to a publication or thesis, is actually more lenient than one might suspect at first. The "serendipity awareness" factor is not easily analyzed, or even defined, but in general it consists of simply knowing enough about your material, and about science in general, so that some important or interesting observation does not slip by unnoticed.

What has been the overall result of this pedagogical exploration, this attempt to take McCommons' advice to heart in biology classes? On city campus, in Biodiversity, where time is limited to six contact hours a week (three of those in lab with a TA), I immediately see those who assimilate information and produce good research problems easily, almost naturally. Their lab instructors tell me about them, then recommend that I recruit them for the field program, or sometimes for honors thesis research. At CPBS we have much more than six hours a week to engage in exploration, so that in Field Parasitology, during evening discussions, students' intellectual maturity grows noticeably over the five-week period, at least if they make an effort to ask conceptually important questions. As a consequence, their daily assignments take on an increasingly sophisticated flavor. Am I able to quantify this change, use an "evaluation instrument" to produce a report that would impress the accountants? No, of course not. Does anyone ever get a perfect score, ten checks? Yes; about once every two or three years—about 2 percent of the people, and about 0.2 percent of the question sets written.

At this point, maybe it would be helpful to actually read some student work. On this particular day in the field, we had done an exercise on larval trematodes in snails, spending many hours collecting several species of snails in various habitats, then dissecting these snails to determine what kinds of parasites they contained. Trematodes are worms that live as adults in vertebrates, but must pass through several developmental stages in other kinds of animals before becoming infective to their final host, usually some vertebrate predator. Cercariae are the larval trematodes that emerge from snails and must infect the next host in order to continue the life cycle. Snails also play host to ectocommensal annelids that live underneath the shell, in the mantle cavity, so when we do a snail exercise, we invariably also deal with these annelids of the genus *Chaetogaster*. The snails are usually of four genera: *Physa, Helisoma, Gyraulus*, and *Stagnicola*. We finished the day, actually well into the evening, by assessing vertebrate use of the sampled habitats, using the cercariae in snails as "indicators" based on published accounts of life cycles. In other words, if a particular type of parasite was found in a snail, then we could infer that a particular kind of vertebrate host—snapping turtle, raccoon, deer, and the like—had visited the site and left behind some feces laced with worm eggs.

Although some of the following questions may well have been answered by parasitologists years ago, the student who wrote them—a junior in college at the time—had no experience with parasites prior to taking the course. Nor did she have access to most of the massive body of literature on larval trematodes. Finally, she was required to base her questions on the previous day's observations, and had only forty-eight hours after that class to generate them. For her, at least, the exercise was pure exploration of a completely unknown system. What follows, with a couple of typos edited, is one of the very few question-sets ever to receive a perfect score of ten "checks." You will discover immediately that they are "nested" sets, in the sense that each question is actually a group of related questions. If any young person decided to answer all of these questions, then the result would be a lifetime of meaningful scientific achievement. They were written by Karen Pearson, turned in on July 23, 1997, and included here with her permission. Ms. Pearson is now a medical student at the University of Iowa.

1. How long is a cercaria able to live outside of a host? It was apparent that the cercariae expended a large amount of energy through movement. How long are they able to maintain this motion? How much total energy is expended in the life cycle of a digenetic parasite in order to reproduce? Do cercariae feed or does all their energy come from stored resources? How and when are these resources acquired?

2. How do the levels of infection vary between the species of snails? Is there a difference in the level of infection between conical and spiral snails? How do the size and age of the snail affect the number of parasites it contains? Does the level of infection increase with age? Do the feeding habits differ between species? How does this affect their level of infection?

3. How does the tail of the cercaria affect its ability to find a host? Are fork-tailed cercariae able to move more rapidly than those without forked tails? Do fin folds allow more directional control? How did these characteristics evolve? Did fin folds and forked tails evolve to improve the chances of finding a host? Did fin folds ever serve a respiratory function?

4. What is the function of the stylet? Is it ever used as a sensory organ when it comes in contact with a possible host? Could a cercaria use it to burrow out of an unsuitable host? Can a stylet function without penetration glands? Does the stylet help the cercaria exit the redia more quickly than a cercaria without a stylet?

5. What other intermediate hosts are used by trematodes besides snails? Could a parasite be more successful due to less competition if it used a different intermediate host? Are trematodes ever host specific with regard to the snails? Are there certain cercariae that can only be found in one species of snail or are the parasites cosmopolitan within the snail population?

6. What function does the spiny collar on the echinostome cercaria serve? Does it help the cercaria penetrate a host? Is it similar in structure and function to a stylet? Is the collar used in attachment or does it function in movement?

7. How does the level of infection of frogs with *Haematoloechus longiplexus* compare with the level of infection of snails in the area with cercariae of *Haematoloechus longiplexus*? How successful are these parasites in this environment? How many cercariae must be released by snails to produce one successful adult lung fluke? How many cercariae actually make it to a host but don't survive?

8. How do environmental factors affect the shedding of cercariae? Are the cercariae able to detect the conditions when they would most likely be able to find a host? Is the timing of the life cycle the same or can it be adjusted according to environmental conditions?

9. What is the relationship between *Chaetogaster* [an ectocommensal annelid] and *Physa* [a genus of snail]? Does the level of infection ever become fatal? Are snails the definitive hosts? How do the snails become infected? Is *Chaetogaster* host specific? Would they ever choose a slug or another gas-

tropod without a shell as a host? Is the shell necessary for protection or is there some nutritional value to the annelid?

10. What function do the large setal bundles serve on a *Chaeto-gaster*? Once a *Chaetogaster* finds a host does it ever move around on the host? Will it ever fall off and have to find another host? At what point during the life cycle does a *Chaetogaster* find a host? Are the setal bundles fully developed at this point? Once a host is found, are the setal bundles used for functions besides movement? Do they aid in attachment?

Ms. Pearson ends her paper with an assessment of her own work: "Question 3 is my best question. It relates the anatomy and physiology of the parasite to its life cycle. It also provides a comparison between different species of cercariae. Another interesting aspect is that it deals with the evolution of various types of cercariae."

What you have just read is a truly superb piece of student work. If Ms. Pearson had been inclined to become a scientist instead of a physician, she would have been a highly successful one. And had she chosen to become an academic scientist, then she would very likely have spent the next three or four decades producing a long string of similarly successful students, at least some of whom would have gone on to productive careers themselves.

What is most revealing, at least to me, about student question sets is the extent to which we fail miserably in teaching some aspects of basic biology, and succeed admirably in teaching others. Because of the nature of our evening field parasitology discussions, my colleagues' "success" often appears as evolutionary paradigms that seem quite consistent with human volition, almost political and economic ideas of competition, benefits, winners and losers. This aspect of Darwinism seems to embed itself easily and deeply into the young mind, almost as if connecting therein with a hard-wired sense of the way the world operates. Thus I often see questions such as: If a host species becomes extinct will the parasite invade another host species? That is a fairly logical question, especially given Americans' tendency to impose their logical systems on nature. In this case the question reveals the underlying idea that if you run out of one resource, you just go get another, a consumer society trait if there ever was one! But it is also a question that ignores the evolutionary biology of sym-biont-host combinations. Parasites are heavily constrained by their history, and over evolutionary time seem to survive in either a single host, or in a group of related host species. If a host becomes extinct, the parasite species' survival depends largely on the mechanism of ex-tinction. For example, if a host becomes extinct because it evolves into another species, the parasite is likely to ride along unchanged. If the host becomes extinct because of some catastrophic event, such as humans clearing a forest, then the parasite's fate will depend largely on its own evolutionary history and the extent to which that history has already given it options such as broad geographical distribution and access to other host species. Students rarely think in these more subtle terms about evolution, at least until they are exposed repeat-edly to the ideas. Whatever else it has accomplished, therefore, the question set reveals what my fellow faculty members are teaching.

This is perhaps a good time to elaborate on the go-around-the-room technique, too. Five points can be made about this little teaching trick. First, it's not very new or innovative; second, it costs virtually nothing; third, it's very rarely used in university classes; fourth, it's a great leveler among students who usually judge one another on traits having nothing to do with intellect; and fifth, it changes the charac-ter of a classroom instantly. Many years after I started using go-around-the-room, I happened upon a wonderful book by A. F. Nixon, entitled *Teaching Biology for Appreciation* (1949). In Lesson 1, in the chapter "Biology and Art," Nixon recommends asking stu-dents to write down the most beautiful things they have experienced pertaining to plants. Then, he continues, "each pupil is called upon to read what he has written." His predictions of what will happen, and where these plant experiences come from, are right on target. "They begin to have their attention directed to beauties in nature. . . . They become interested in what others consider beautiful." and "Many of the things listed will be plants grown at home . . . in general, things not in the immediate environment of all." In today's university class-room, Nixon's expectations seem antiquated at best, terminally naive at worst. Correctly, and appropriately, however, he concludes, "The time is not spent in vain."

In my experience, go-around-the-room is such a powerful tool because it levels the interactions among peers by placing a premium on their intellectual contributions. When every student must present, and each must provide a different question, problem, or assessment, then leadership temporarily passes to those with the most interesting ideas. You can never predict who these people will be, at least from looking at them. I'd be lying if I said there was no element of competition in this activity, but the competition is not very heated or destructive. The most common reaction among students is "he took my question!" whereupon the student whose turn is coming up begins searching his/her question supply for a new [better?] one. In Field Parasitology I start at a different place in class every time we do this kind of discussion, and I always retain the right to have the last comment about each student's contribution. When the subject is as complex as symbiont biology, then it's fairly easy to make every person's ideas important.

How do I use this trick in a large auditorium of introductory students? I hand the portable microphone to someone, then instead of go-around-the-room we go-down-the-row. In such a setting, the microphone itself is highly empowering, if for no other reason than that the portable mike is such an ingrained part of the popular music and video scene and the sound commands attention. The first time through, I usually have to remind students to hold the mike right up to their mouth, "like a rock star." One by one, their voices, their logic, and their rationale are laid out for everyone to hear, and share. As an instructor, I have the opportunity to demonstrate patience, reinforce students' ideas, and point out the positive and educational components of what they've said, then thank them for their contributions. This kind of interaction alters the very character of a large lecture section class.

Finally, what does the question-set do to the student-teacher relationship? Because these questions are of a totally different nature from those typically asked (e.g., in class during or after a lecture), the student-teacher roles are altered, if not reversed. In other words, the student is giving careful thought to what's been accomplished in the educational activity, then extrapolating from that relatively short activity into a long-term intellectual commitment. This is exactly what practicing scientists do. A faculty member may not have to actually answer any of the questions on a student's set, but he or she is obliged to respond to these questions in some way. Both student and teacher know the questions cannot be answered immediately with received wisdom or by authority, but instead the research must actually be done. This mutual understanding of what is involved in obtaining an answer makes those involved become colleagues rather than students and teachers. In a go-around-the-room follow-up, the teacher is one of those in the circle. However, the teacher also has the benefit of research experience, so usually is able to find something to compliment in each student's contribution. Even if a student's question is not a particularly good one, we can always talk about the logistics of doing the research, the appropriate systems for addressing the problem, and what the results might be. In the final analysis, therefore, the teacher gives up power—an immediate manifestation of which is the difficult question—and the student gains intellectual stature and, hopefully, confidence to seek more stature. Asymmetry between student and faculty is reduced or eliminated, such elimination being an empowering pedagogical goal that all of us try to achieve, but few of us ever do achieve, on city campus.

Elimination of the asymmetry in any student/faculty relationship is, I honestly believe, a key element in teaching at all levels. The archtypical intellectual tyrant who imposes his or her mind-set, research objectives and interests, and (ultimately) social behavior, on his or her students is a case in point. Every department at a major university has such people. In the sciences, their lives typically are governed by their grants, which, in turn, get renewed only if certain kinds and volumes of work get done. Because grant dollars are easy to count and overhead return enhances middle management's image of itself, these grant dollars, and the programs that generate them, are usually considered indications of quality. Only rarely does anyone ever ask whether a scientist has produced a good problem-seeker, or to what extent an individual has actually empowered his/her students. Yet the most successful mentors seem to do just that, usually by giving away to their students not only good questions, but also proprietary rights to the research problems derived from these questions. In all fairness, of course, grant money doesn't necessarily pre-

vent scientists from being so generous, and many well-funded programs also produce excited, well-rounded, productive progeny. But
there is no necessary link between money and mentoring talent, so
the opposite also occurs, and with surprising regularity. What a true
teacher needs is a supply of people, enough knowledge, challenging
and easily accessible material, and a long long list of questions.

8

A PROJECT

*I'd go in there and build a dam from one side of that valley to the other
and stop the goddamned waste!*
—William Mulholland, describing what he would do to
Yosemite National Park (from Marc Reisner, *Cadillac Desert*)

Chapter 7, Questions, begins with the assertion that outside of art classes, few students in America's public schools are ever asked what they would like to study, but instead are told what to study. I have no way of proving this claim to be true, but for the past twenty-eight years I have asked field station students what they would like to study, and from watching their responses, have come to the conclusion that they've rarely (if ever) been asked that question. In this case, the "what to study" is a parasitological concept, disguised as a research project of their own choosing—an original exploration of some natural phenomenon. The "study" is actually a test of our assumptions about the way that nature operates. Because students only have about a month (shortened to about two weeks in 2003) to accomplish their research, from idea to presentation, these projects routinely become a search for pattern from which one can infer a process. Most of the time, their final inference could be the basis for a doctoral dissertation.

For example, we might easily assume that as fish become older, they continue to acquire, thus accumulate, parasites, so that larger fish would be more heavily infected than smaller ones. This assumption is actually a statement about the way natural systems work—the mechanism by which apparent order is established. Conversely, we could just as easily assume that as fish age they either die from their parasites or become immune, so that a sample of older fish would have fewer parasites than a sample of younger fish. Either of these predictions could be tested—in this case using the same data set— thus both are, in fact, scientific hypotheses, and they are derived from our sense of what to expect when we observe nature closely. We tend to impose order on nature, however, so it would be a little discomforting to discover that there is no relationship whatsoever between the age of a fish and the abundance of its parasites. But to an scientist, no pattern is a pattern just as zero is a number, and failure to find anticipated order in nature simply means we must look for organizing mechanisms other than those on our current list of possibilities. Or, we must admit that perhaps counter to our very human view of the world, no permanent organizing mechanisms are at work.

It really does not take very much time or effort to test either of these hypotheses about fish and their parasites, and indeed we have done it numerous times as a class. We simply go to the river, collect fish, measure and dissect them, put their tissues under the microscope, and identify their parasites as best we can. This task usually requires about an hour to an hour and a half per fish, so that a class of twenty students usually can process forty minnows in an afternoon. By the time we add a trip to the river, one or two hours spent saving specimens for making permanent slides, the statistical analysis, and discussion, we've spent twelve class hours, or 240 person hours total. For a pair of students who have never undertaken a project before, this class activity could also become a legitimate training exercise, and the 240 person hours represent three weeks of full time work for the two of them. Forty-hour weeks are a myth at any field station, of course, or for researchers in general, so in taking on such a project, our two budding scientists might well have their first encounter with the logistical adventures associated with the study of natural systems. In addition, a single collection is never enough because scientific observations must be confirmed before being considered valid, so the collection, dissection, identification, and quantification must be repeated, hopefully several times.

Both of the foregoing hypotheses about fish and their symbionts address a preconceived idea about the natural world—that parasites are always "out there" in nature, perhaps even as something harmful, or at least undesirable. The fact that these fish are likely to have more than one kind of parasite, each with its own particular distribution among the fish population, further complicates the issue, especially for the student. What happens if the first hypothesis—that fish acquire parasites as they age—is true for one species of parasitic worm but not for another in the same species of fish in the same locality? Or, conversely, that the second hypothesis is true only for certain host-parasite combinations and not for others? In these cases, which are fairly typical of the field station experience, our search for pattern has yielded information that affronts our inclination to generalize about things we do not understand, for example, a relationship between two species. Suddenly there is diversity, not only of kind, but also of process, in a system we perceived as homogeneous. And just as suddenly, this hypothesis-testing exercise reveals that the problem of community assembly and organization is much larger and much more complex than at first envisioned.

What I have just outlined, indirectly, are the pedagogical reasons for doing research, regardless of the subject, and probably regardless of whether a particular project has been done before, so long as a student is ignorant of previous results. Of all the role-playing opportunities in field programs, the independent project is perhaps the most legitimate. In science, original investigation is at least somewhat formalized regardless of the topic, so that part of this legitimacy comes from having to think and act like a scientist regardless of the burden imposed on great ideas by uncooperative animals, bad weather, unusually wet (or dry) years, burned-out microscope lamps, or ruined computer discs. However, at a biological field station, there is a more important, albeit subtle, aspect of a student's independent study, namely, the source of the project itself.

In the preceding example, we assumed a seemingly logical relationship between parts of nature then reduced that assumption to a specific hypothesis about fish and worms, which we then tested. Such a sequence of behavior is standard fare in science, and indeed is deeply embedded in our practice. Thomas Kuhn (*The Structure of Scientific Revolutions*) refers to this approach as the "normal science" of using accepted paradigms as our framework for investigation. Richard McCommons (see Chapter 7) would describe it as problem-solving rather than problem-seeking. In increasingly unflattering evaluations, a figure skater might refer to it as "doing school figures," and an acerbic artist on a bad day might consider it "janitorial work" —cleaning up intellectually after someone else who made a mess of things by finding a good problem. But in the field we have an alternative to school figures and intellectual housecleaning, namely nature itself.

The alternative to normal science is seen in the manner that one finds projects. As a graduate student once said to me after coming back from some large national scientific meetings, "they have all these grand ideas about the way the world is suppose to work, then go looking for systems to test them. You parasitologists just go out there and start looking around, asking who's infected with whom, discovering all these systems, and eventually you find good problems." (Brant, personal communication) Her point was that in my lab we tended to let nature tell us how it might be operating then use that information to determine the structure of our more formal studies. An excellent example of this approach can be found in a study done by a student named Molly Weichman, who eventually published her work in the *Journal of Parasitology*. Her story is an easily understood illustration of how one "finds" a problem by starting with undirected, or perhaps I should say curiosity-directed, rather than theory-directed, exploration.

Molly was one of the top students in my Biodiversity course one spring, and the next fall she came by to ask about doing an honors project in my lab. Undergraduates usually start by learning all the techniques we use, and in the process of doing that, also get exposed to the various systems we use in our research. These systems consist primarily of protistan parasites in insects and microscopic worms on small fish. I started working on these systems a long time ago because they were cheap, abundant, and provided a seemingly inexhaustible supply of conceptually important projects, not only for me, but also for my students. Molly decided very quickly that she did not like working with insects, so we got in my truck and went seining for minnows in one of the local streams.

The first stream we looked at was a place called West Oak Creek, and it was chosen because a young man named Aaron McCormick, a graduate student in Brent Nickol's lab, had taken me there some months earlier. Brent Nickol is another parasitologist, and his research all centers on the biology of thorny-headed worms, or Acanthocephala. Aaron was looking specifically for creek chubs, *Semotilus atromaculatus*, which were not infected with these worms, so he could use them in experimental infections. Asking me, a faculty member, to help him seine fish is fairly typical of our operation. Aaron had been a student at Camelot, so it was quite normal for him to assume an interest shared between faculty and student, a willingness to help one another, and an ornery love of water and mud. This was clearly a case in which a field-program behavior had been successfully exported! We quickly collected a bucket of minnows of several species in addition to creek chubs, and back in the lab I took the ones Aaron didn't want. From an examination of these fish, I knew there was a great deal of material just waiting for some student who wanted to get out of the lab periodically and who didn't mind working on small fish. Molly turned out to be that person.

Like most young people who first start trying to isolate the microscopic worms that live on minnow gills, Molly struggled with the first few fish, but before long she was able to get the worms on slides and make videotape of their hooks and other sclerotized parts. We went back through the tapes as a follow-up to her identification attempts, and noted that there seemed to be more than one species of parasite present. This kind of observation is not at all unusual, indeed it is to be expected. A rather paradigmatic reaction to these worms would have been to assume competition between the species then seek to demonstrate it—not ask *whether* they were interacting, but ask *how* they were interacting. This sort of intellectual approach to ectoparasites on minnow gills is a perfect, albeit pretty minor, illustration of Thomas Kuhn's main thesis; in other words, it's normal science. Molly was not particularly interested in testing someone else's paradigms, however (think janitorial work), so she kept on searching for problems, always asking what she could do with this system consisting of the fathead minnow, *Pimephales promelas*, and the microscopic parasites on its gills, all living in a prairie stream subject to extremely variable flow caused by a variety of factors including beavers and thunderstorms. It was a thunderstorm that showed Molly her problem.

West Oak Creek was too high and muddy to get into one day, so we drove around for a couple of miles looking for another site, eventually stopping by a bridge over Elk Creek. After climbing down steep and heavily overgrown banks, we managed to find a pool filled with fathead minnows, and in a few minutes collected enough for a few days' work. By this time, Molly was adept at dissections and was ready to use her skills on something more challenging than demonstrating the presence of a worm. Not long after we got back to the lab, Molly mentioned that in contrast to her West Oak Creek minnows, the fish from Elk Creek had black spots on them. These spots turned out to be the larval stages of a trematode species that lives as an adult in fish-eating birds, primarily kingfishers. Thus a parasite was being transmitted to kingfishers through the fish of one local stream, but not through that same species of fish in another stream.

A quick check of the map showed that the two streams merged about a mile away from Molly's two collecting sites. Suddenly she had a hypothesis: fish swam freely throughout a prairie stream system. The "tool" that allowed her to test this assertion about the way nature worked was the larval parasite. The black spot was a form of natural marker that identified fish from Elk Creek. All she had to do was repeat her collections several times over the course of a year, applying the knowledge gained from her serendipitous look at Elk Creek minnows. If the fish swam freely throughout the drainage, then there should be no significant statistical differences between the frequency of black spots on fish collected in the various streams and their tributaries. But if fish were restricted to particular parts of the drainage, then these differences would be significant.

Molly's original decision to walk into my office resulted in field trips, collections, hundreds of hours at the microscope, long days in the library dealing with original literature, equally long days at the computer doing statistical analysis, a presentation at a regional scientific meeting, several drafts of a manuscript, revision of that manuscript according to comments by anonymous reviewers, and eventual publication in an international, peer-reviewed, scientific journal (Weichman and Janovy, 1999). In other words, she found a project and carried it through to closure. Then she got married and went off to medical school. But as with the students discussed in the next chapter, Molly's project gave her a kind of education she could never have obtained in the classroom alone. She was fortunate in having some nearby streams as her laboratory, and in retrospect one might conclude that access to natural areas is a prerequisite for meaningful research. But if we are going to build an educational Eden, then Molly's experience must be generalized to subjects beyond biology and to places far beyond the Salt Valley Watershed west of Lincoln, Nebraska.

How do we extend the empowering properties of an individual science project into the typical university classroom, or any classroom, for that matter? It seems to me that there are three important factors that must be present in any teacher's attempt to address this question. First, whatever the student produces must become his or her possession. In our lab, we always refer to various projects as the *student's*— Adam's research, Heidi's project, Wendy's work, or Adam's paper, Heidi's presentation, Wendy's slides. This feature of our student-level independent study—namely—possession is borrowed directly from the visual arts: painting, sculpture, photography. In the visual arts, time is budgeted for personal and original work, and over the course of a year, a student generates a portfolio and develops both a style and an intellectual focus that is his or her own. Furthermore, a good art teacher encourages and promotes this development, and if the teacher is a really good one, then the student's peers do the same.

When it comes to developing this idea of possession, therefore, Eden is not in western Nebraska, but as close as the nearest art department. One never finds this possession of one's own product in a typical science class, although it's an attribute of everyday studio art. Instead, "knowledge" always remains the property of science itself, whose local representative is the teacher. I suspect that such ownership is also characteristic of history, economics, and engineering, and I believe that this situation stifles student originality in those disciplines the same way it does in science. The teacher's task—at once very simple but also quite difficult—is to give the student something that is highly individual, something that the teacher can comment on but cannot own. Better yet, this item should be something that the teacher respects and values, but doesn't care to own. I know that in my Biodiversity class, for example, photocopies of five journal articles, each describing a new species, works very well as that "something." Obviously nobody "owns" original species descriptions, but someone can "own" a unique combination of five, such ownership coming not only from the intended use of those papers, but more important, from the way the combination was assembled. Some combination of desire, interest, and logistics drives the selection of the five descriptions. Surely other disciplines have their equivalents of original species descriptions, all as handy as a local library.

The second important factor of project work is self-acknowledged "failure," and subsequent revision. Again, the visual arts provide our most accessible example, although creative writing and music composition courses are also good places to experience this second characteristic of learning how to learn. The subject is irrelevant in this case. What is relevant is the act of doing an original piece of work, standing back and assessing that work's quality from several perspectives, then making decisions to modify the work. Writing is ideal for such purposes because it can be modified over and over again, especially today with word-processing programs, with little cost. Marble sculpture works just as well, but the logistics are relatively daunting, especially to a college sophomore. Thus we might ask the question: What characteristics do sculpturing in marble, painting in watercolor, writing poetry, and describing a new species of parasite from the intestine of beetles have in common?

The answer would be cycles of attempt, subsequent realization that something was not being done to the artist's (scientist's) satisfaction, then repetition with change in approach. Artists and writers who don't learn to accept a certain level of failure early on don't continue to produce original work for very long. Again, these elements of original work—so typical of daily professional life—are largely missing from any typical science class, and probably from university classes in general. What's important in this exercise is the focus on a single project, a single paper, one endeavor, repeated over and over again. In this instance, intellectual work becomes the equivalent of serious athletic practice, and the teacher assumes the role of coach instead of pundit (Adler, 1982). Any smart coach knows that words of encouragement, a sharing of goals, are as essential to the teaching effort as words of correction. Thus at any university, every offensive lineman is doing exactly what every biology student ought to be doing—working at the same task over and over again, trying to perfect it, assessing his own strengths and weaknesses. Every time our right tackle takes the field, he asks how he should be playing.

Because offensive linemen are notoriously intelligent, however, eventually this lineman is sure to rephrase his question into a more general form: How should right tackle be played? At this point, the lineman is no longer asking how *he* should play football, but instead asking *what is football?* This evolution in the form of our athlete's basic question is what needs to be *taken beyond* the practice field. As a student grows in sophistication, therefore, the cycles of self-evaluation and correction will start to include assessment of the work's conceptual contribution—the extent to which a project is *about* football instead *of* football, *about* art instead *of* art, or *about* parasitology instead *of* parasitology. We rarely if ever find this second factor—an ongoing cycle of personal evaluation, revision, and conceptual assessment of one's own work—in typical science classes. We never seem to get from the "of" stage to the "about" stage.

The third critical factor of project work is acknowledgement of the fact that projects serve primarily as sources of problems rather than as sources of solutions. This fundamental property of research is typically lost on taxpayers, who usually believe, and often demand, that research should be "focused," "useful," or "productive." In other words, we want researchers to cure cancer, develop an AIDS vaccine, and build a SUV that gets 100mpg in town and accelerates from 0 to 60 in 8.3 seconds. But that's not the way science works, and anyone who's both doing and teaching science knows it. That's also not the way art, music, history, economics, sociology, English literature, and philosophy work, as anyone who both practices and teaches those disciplines can attest. Only engineering seeks to operate in this focused manner on "useful" projects, but engineers too, just like scientists, usually fail to satisfy the taxpayer ideals (see the preceding chapter's discussion on "success" rates for those doing anything original, p. 89.). On the other hand, most engineers succeed admirably because they find lots of work just by doing their work.

Why all this so-called failure to achieve practical goals? Perhaps the most explanatory metaphor is that of the island of understanding in the sea of ignorance. The shoreline of this island is the interface between what we know and what we don't know, between that information we can actually put to good use, and that unexplored body of information that has plenty of potential for changing the way we do business—if we only knew about it. What happens when we do research—that is—conduct a project? Hopefully by the time that project is finished, we've increased our understanding and our island has gotten larger. But our shoreline has also increased, thus so has the length of our boundary between understanding and ignorance.

Area of this metaphorical island increases exponentially, however, while perimeter length increases linearly, so understanding should gain rapidly against ignorance. And admittedly, scientists and engineers have produced, and continue to produce, a steady stream of perfectly amazing gadgets, our use of which is redefining the term "human being." Yes, indeed, we are getting better educated about many things. But even as our technological power is increasing exponentially, we encounter a seemingly endless supply of baffling and difficult problems anywhere we look, from the outer fringes of the universe to our daily newspaper headlines to the molecular landscapes of DNA. What is the source of this paradox, and why didn't we discover everything there is to discover about our environment and ourselves a long time ago and quit doing research?

Perhaps the best explanation is that the volume of research and development, especially in areas thought profitable, is simply enormous. Thus our so-called island of understanding has become a very large and complex one, metaphorically speaking, and our technological power lets us see a universe that is far larger, and far smaller, than we ever imagined. This is a good time to point out that this metaphoral island may share some properties with real islands, as postulated by the classic work of MacArthur and Wilson (1967), entitled, appropriately enough, *The Theory of Island Biogeography*. MacArthur and Wilson claimed that large, complex islands support a far greater number of species than do small simple islands. This principle has been applied to isolated patches of various kinds and sizes regardless of their physical makeup, for example, parcels of woodland in a predominately row-crop landscape. There is no inherent reason why this principle should not also apply to islands of understanding in seas of ignorance, with large, complex areas of intellectual endeavor supporting rich communities made up mostly of ideas and innovations. Perhaps at a certain stage of intellectual development, societies begin to look more like oceans than islands, and "pockets" of ignorance begin to form within a field of endeavor, then take on the character of "internal islands." The last paragraph is a perfect example of what we would call Big Talk (see Chapter 11).

Finally, we might ask what is the real product of research? What is to be gained by a asking a student to actually do an original study? The real product of research is an educated individual, one who has been "taught" by two teachers that are nothing more than emergent phenomena. These teachers are "the discipline" and "nature," or for nonbiologists, "nature-equivalents." In the case of young scientists, the discipline is actually the whole structure of science—the practices, history, outlets for publication, appropriate technology, and existing paradigms, as well as the individuals who are exerting current influence in a particular specialty. Nature, as I've indicated elsewhere (see Chapter 9), can be an especially effective but unforgiving teacher. No single teacher can convey everything that students will learn from firsthand interactions with both the discipline and the material subject of his or her research. The single teacher can, however, thrust students into this larger world of original investigation, then pass along the fruits of experience consisting mainly of a certain calmness in the face of both success and failure.

Human teachers don't necessarily teach students how to actually do research. Instead, we give away good problems then get out of the way, helping mostly when asked. By "give away" I mean give away *everything* associated with a project—the physical labor, the data analysis, the tedium, the writing, the responsibility for graphics, but most of all, the credit. Granted, when I supply the room, the microscopes, whatever chemicals may be required, the regulatory compliance for safety training, hazardous materials inventory and disposal, and animal care, glassware, Internet access, a key to my office and lab, and a certain sense of how to be a professional, then I expect my name to go on a paper as the second or third author. But the student's name always goes first on any publication that results from student work.

Does this original study have to be "important"? No, not at all. In fact, when projects are chosen for their instructional power instead of their glamour or "importance," the more likely they are to sound pretty arcane, if not outright useless and dumb to the proverbial person on the street. Consider some titles of recent presentations in the Field Parasitology course:

1. A study of differences in parasite diversity at various ages among *Fundulus zebrinus* and *Notropis ludibundus* (Megan Hylok).
2. The impact of *Posthodiplostomum minimum* metacercariae upon the reproductive success of the plains killifish *Fundulus zebrinus* (Mark Boggy and Justin Kauk).
3. Distribution of monogeneans on the gills of *Lepomis macrochirus* (Centrarchidae) (Charles Randel and Chad Lee).
4. Comparative analysis of Branchiobdellida assemblages from a population of *Orconectes immunes* and *Orconectes viriles* (Brandan Lubken and Rick Grimm).

Are any of these studies likely to make a major difference in the economic health of Nebraska? No. Will they result in a cure for cancer? No, of course not. Will they be featured in the university's promo spot at halftime of a nationally televised football game? Dumb question. But did the time and effort spent compiling the data to write a fifteen-page paper and give a ten-minute presentation completely, and permanently, alter the thought processes of the individuals whose names are listed behind the titles? Yes. I, like any other teacher who has ever "guided" the independent study of a student just starting his or her first original research, can unequivocally vouch for the transforming effect this experience has on the participants—teacher and student alike. The real products of this research are the people who did it. The history of science is relatively clear on this point: produce enough scientists and give them enough support and opportunity to follow their curiosity, and society reaps the benefits—economic and technological benefits, the products of innovation, and an altered standard of living. Thus it is of absolutely no importance whatsoever to society that Brandon and Rick spent many intense days doing a comparative analysis of Branchiobdellida assemblages from populations of a couple of crayfish species—*Orconectes immunes* and *Orconectes viriles*. It is, however, of vital importance that thousands of Brandons and Ricks everywhere are doing something original, on their own, that could easily sound equally as inconsequential.

9

UNDOMESTICATED SYSTEMS

The Call of the Wild
—Jack London

A domesticated system is a species that can be bred in the laboratory, standardized in terms of size, age, or physiological conditions, and made to produce predictable supplies of teaching or research material on schedule. In the case of parasites, a domesticated system must include not only the parasite, but also its host, and both must be capable of being standardized and manipulated. In spite of their scientific name (*Felis domesticus*), housecats are not themselves very domesticated, so the name is probably a misnomer. A cat-tapeworm combination is probably more of a domesticated system than the cat alone because tapeworm numbers can be manipulated, and the worms are long-lived, so that the two organisms together average out higher on the manipulation scale than the cat by itself. Of course in this reference to housecats I'm being somewhat facetious, although cats easily become feral—indicating the ease with which they revert to the wild state—and a single infected cat could supply tapeworm eggs daily for months on end, probably more reliably than it could supply affection and obedience. As for helminth parasites, the rat tapeworm, *Hymenolepis diminuta*, is perhaps the most studied and most well understood, simply because both it and its host can be bred, standardized, and manipulated so easily in the lab. The rat-*H. diminuta* combination is an excellent example of a domesticated system.

The most sophisticated biological research depends entirely on domesticated systems. The intestinal bacterium, *Escherichia coli*, may well be the most domesticated organism known to biologists, although the fruit fly (*Drosophila melanogaster*), corn (*Zea mays*), and the microscopic nematode (*Coenorhabtidis elegans*), are all close behind. Science has made major strides toward understanding fundamental life processes because of our ability to manipulate these organisms and use them to test hypotheses about cellular function and genetic control of development. In every case the organisms reproduce readily in the laboratory, and exhibit genetic variations that can be isolated into separate strains by selective breeding. Most important, however, is that these particular species do things for an investigator that he or she cannot always do alone—synthesize a particular mutant protein upon demand.

The vast and overwhelming majority of biological systems are not domesticated, however, and of this number, most will never be "brought into the lab," as we say in the business. Parasites are particularly wild because their nutritional requirements and immediate physiological environments must be met and supplied by the host, typically also a wild animal. Even though one can guess at the nutritional needs of most animals, including parasites, the delicately balanced environment typically required by endosymbionts can only rarely be supplied in a petri dish. Thus our success at culturing parasites apart from their hosts has been extremely limited. We need the rat in order to maintain *Hymenolepis diminuta*, and the very word "rat" implies an extraordinarily complex set of biochemical reactions and products, all maintained in wonderful stability through evolved homeostatic mechanisms. Therefore the rat can do things for us that we cannot do on the lab bench—namely—grow a tapeworm from larva to reproducing adult. Although the adult worm has been the primary focus of parasitologists, in practice, we also need roaches or beetles to eat the *H. diminuta* eggs and so produce infective larvae. The roach that serves as an intermediate host—a source of tapeworm for the rat—also does things we cannot do for ourselves—grow an infective tapeworm larva from an egg picked up in rat feces.

During the first day at Cedar Point, a student encounters at least a dozen undomesticated systems, and is encouraged to start thinking of at least some of them as project material. This experience alone can be considered an intellectual "baptism by fire." Suddenly instead of being able to manipulate a system in the lab, as the hypothesis-test model of science teaches young people to do, a student must first begin thinking about ways the organisms can show him or her something about the way nature operates. Probably the surest route to "failure" in this first encounter—failure being the inability to actually conduct a project from start to finish—is to assume that the organisms can be brought back to a laboratory and kept alive for some length of time. The second most guaranteed route to failure is to assume that these organisms will be available at a particular collecting site for any three-week period. As pointed out so magnificently in the French film *Microcosmos*, to most of the world's animals, averaging about a half inch in length, days can be like years to us, and a month is often a lifetime. Anyone who goes to the field must adjust his or her internal clock to that of this tiny natural world.

In this first brush with reality, the particular species involved are not as important as their commonness and their wildness are. For example, certain aquatic insects and small crustaceans are exceedingly abundant in easily accessible habitats, yet are also notoriously uncooperative. The major criteria for good student project organisms— numbers, accessibility, participation in a symbiotic relationship, a life that can reveal, or at least suggest, the mechanisms that regulate such participation—are all met by such creatures. But the one criterion that seems to characterize science in the minds of textbook writers, namely our ability to test a hypothesis by conducting an experiment, is not. A person might be able to do experiments, but the efforts to accomplish this goal take two forms: one, field experiments using such devices as inclusion and exclusion cages; and two, a long, usually arduous and unsuccessful battle to bring organisms into the lab and make them reproduce on a human's schedule.

In my view, students of biology, regardless of their level, and regardless of their ultimate professional goals, must learn how truly wild most species are. I'm not downplaying the fundamental importance of what we've learned about life from studying fruit flies and *C. elegans*. On the other hand, neither am I conceding that the experimental hypothesis-test model of science, *dependent as it is on domesticated systems*, is a true reflection of the state of our science—biology. Much biology is studied in the same general way detectives approach a crime scene. Biologists look for evidence and draw inferences. Then they look for more evidence, and if they find it, they may modify their inferences. Eventually they make predictions (testable hypotheses) about the way their system operates and devise various means—including, in some cases, experiments—to test these predictions. Unlike humans, however, no wild plant or animal actually confesses to anything, so the science of biology is often left with unproven, but heavily supported, and even widely accepted, ideas. The central unifying theme of biology—evolution—is an excellent example of this epistemological principle. Depending on the system being studied, biologists can sometimes control all of that system part of the time, or part of it all of the time. When this happy event occurs, then our biologists are able to do some kind of an experiment. But the biology teacher who starts a bunch of freshmen out on experimentation as the only, or even the predominant, model of science, is not doing anybody any favors.

This is probably a good time to examine in detail the encounters between a few students and their undomesticated systems. What are some of the projects involving these systems that have worked reasonably well, at least scientifically, in the field, and why did they work? For any of my former students who may be reading this book, I submit that regardless of how well your projects may have worked scientifically, virtually all the ones that you tried to do worked pedagogically. Of course, your reasons for doing these studies were quite different from my reasons for doing research. I do research to satisfy my curiosity, to keep myself in shape intellectually, to provide a source of problems for the students who ask to work in my lab, and because I simply love the animals involved. Some of my colleagues do research in order to get grants and publish in *Nature,* but that's their problem. Students, particularly in classes that require projects, perform independent investigations in order to find out what it's like doing research. The teacher's job is to make sure they have a legitimate experience—that is—that they take their lumps at the hands of some system. Students need to walk out of the encounter with a chunk of their naiveté missing. When a student looks back on a class project and says, unprompted, "here's what I would do differently next time," then the teacher has succeeded.

To illustrate the struggles with undomesticated systems, I would like to describe three student projects, two of which worked very well scientifically, and the third of which did not work at all, then analyze these projects in terms of their instructional value. All three projects involved some exceedingly wild systems, namely sunfish and the worms that live on their gills. The three students are Megan Collins (BS, UNL, 2000), Adam Brosz (BS, UNL, 2002), and Heidi Baumert (BS, UNL, 2002). All three did their honors theses in my laboratory. Megan and Adam had sunfish projects that were brought to completion in the sense that they eventually got submitted for publication to an international peer-reviewed journal. Heidi's sunfish project had to be abandoned, the first and only such abandonment in my thirty-six years of advising undergraduates doing honors thesis research in my lab. To her credit, Heidi switched projects and although the second one was also difficult, involving even more uncooperative and mysterious animals, she actually brought it to closure. Heidi and Adam are now in medical school; Megan is a graduate student at another university and will eventually be a university professor.

Megan began by asking whether small ectoparasitic worms were host-specific: in other words, was one species of parasite restricted to one species of fish? The fish she chose to study were all members of the sunfish family, Centrarchidae. This family is native to North America and includes not only the familiar bluegill and largemouth bass, but also a number of other common species that are the favorites of young anglers. The parasites were all members of the Monogenoidea ("monogenes"), beautiful but very tiny flatworms with hooks and anchors at their posterior ends, and often-elaborate copulatory structures located in the anterior third of their bodies. The particular group of monogenes she studied was in the subfamily Ancyrocephalinae; there are about ninety species in this subfamily, reported from centrarchid fishes. Sunfish are great aquarium fish; they live for years and eat readily. Although it is possible to rear sunfish in the lab (commercial hatcheries and some scientists do it), the logistics are fairly daunting. The parasites are virtually impossible to domesticate. So the monogene-sunfish combination is not only undomesticated, it's very likely too wild ever to be domesticated, and certainly not in the same way as is the rat-tapeworm system. Thus, Megan could never do an experimental infection.

Therefore, in order to address her question, she had to ask what nature could, and would, tell her about itself. She began by assuming what she'd read in books was correct, namely that certain species of parasites occurred on particular species of fish, then went into the field to find out if the books were correct. Fortunately, Megan also had some insight and a bunch of isolated ponds; the ponds contained various combinations of sunfish species. Her predictions were (1) if a parasite was host-specific in one pond, then it would be host-specific everywhere; (2) if the literature claimed a parasite occurred on a particular fish species, then it would, in fact, occur on that species if given the opportunity; and (3) the mix of fish species in a particular pond would not alter the presumably-evolved patterns of host specificity. To test her predictions, she had to dissect 200 fish, prepare and identify over 1100 parasites each about 0.02 inches long; measure the hooks on all these worms; and, perform extensive statistical analysis using spreadsheets with over 13,000 entries.

What Megan actually discovered is not particularly important to this discussion, although it was important to her and to biology. She presented her results at two regional meetings as well as a national scientific society meeting, and she won the student paper competition at one of the regional meetings. After two rounds of anonymous peer reviews and revisions, her paper was accepted for publication in the *Journal of Parasitology* (Collins and Janovy, 2003). In the process Megan discovered how much discipline it took to finish a piece of research. She also learned how willing her lab companions were to engage in big talk, how to meet the logistical demands of science, and how to meet the social demands of a significant other. She learned to do statistical analysis, write a ten-minute presentation, prepare graphics, operate audiovisual equipment, address problems perceived by anonymous reviewers, and answer questions in public from senior scientists. As for her research results, maybe five people in the world at most really care, or ever will care, that *Haplocleidus dispar* occurs only on black bass in Beckius Pond but on both bluegill and bass in Humphrey Pond. Before her career as a university professor is over, however, thousands, perhaps even tens of thousands, of students, will benefit enormously from what Megan Collins learned at the hands of an undomesticated system.

On the surface, Heidi's project should have been the most readily done, and had she obtained the results we expected, the paper would easily have been published. The monogenes on sunfish have a fairly wide variety of holdfast organs, each comprised of small hooks, larger anchors, and the surrounding tissue, collectively called an *opisthaptor*, or simply *haptor*. Heidi asked whether the manner of attachment was related to the structure of the holdfast organ. This question had never been addressed in detail for freshwater fish, but it was a reasonably important question because on a microscopic scale, fish gill surfaces are quite elaborate. Heidi's problem was really about the comparative relationships between related organisms and their common environment; in other words, it was a very nice problem in functional morphology with evolutionary overtones. The research techniques were exceedingly common, standard, and relatively simple. She would make histological sections at two angles, then use these sections to study the worms' attachment under the microscope at a magnification of 1000×. She expected to see exactly how each hook and anchor embedded itself in the gill epithelium, and she expected to see differences between worm species. What she did not expect was that her standard, proven, histological techniques would not work for her.

To section tissues, the materials must first be fixed in a solution of something like formaldehyde, picric acid, and alcohol. This fixation precipitates all the structures in place, down to the cell nuclei and other organelles. The tissue is then dehydrated, using alcohol solutions to remove the water. The alcohol is removed by soaking the tissue in an organic solvent such as xylene, which, in turn, is soluble in molten paraffin. From the xylene, the tissue is placed in paraffin, and from there put into a block and allowed to harden. The paraffin block is put into a machine called a microtome, and slices 0.0004 inch thick of the embedded tissue are cut from the block, one at a time. In the best of all worlds, these slices form a ribbon as they come off the knife, so that they become "serial sections." From these sections, one can then reconstruct the three-dimensional structure of cells and tissues, including—Heidi assumed—gill epithelium and attached worms. She seined the local ponds and came home with plenty of heavily infected fish. Like all beginning scientists, by this time she had learned that good ideas are the easy part of research, collection of your material is the fun part, and then comes the lab work, the tedium, and the waiting.

A thousand slides and many weeks later, Heidi decided that this simple, elegant, straightforward piece of research, using common materials and long-tested techniques, would not yield an honors thesis. Why not? Because for some reason, the worms simply did not (would not?) appear in her gill tissue sections. We then began a study of the so-called "long-tested techniques" themselves, tracing the fate and condition of her tissues through all the processing. Using a heated glass plate in order to keep her paraffin melted under a microscope, she watched her worms and gill pieces through every step of the way. The monogenes were there, attached as they should be, right up to the moment the tissues were put into the paraffin block. After that, because the paraffin became solidified and opaque, nothing could be seen until a day or two later when the sections were stained and the slides became dry enough to examine under the microscope. Hour after hour she sat, looking at the thinly sliced, beautifully stained folds of sunfish gills. Slide after slide yielded nothing. The wilderness would not be brought into the laboratory, would not reveal its secrets even when tried-and-true methods were applied. At some point, it becomes time to walk away from a great idea. There is a ritual, a cleansing, that occurs when such a decision is made. Tissues go into the garbage disposal, paraffin goes back into the oven for recycling, slides get tossed into the broken glass container, and a new notebook gets purchased. But you never forget the experience; and you never stop wondering why that great idea could not be bent into submission.

There is a standing joke among biology professors that all your former students are either bartenders or physicians. A few of them become professional scientists, of course, but at any large university the vast majority of the young people you encounter are headed for medical school. In a more sober vein, we also sometimes admit anticipating that time in the future when we look up from a hospital bed and see a familiar face—a "kid" we had in class.

At that point, we trust that the student will have acquired all of the standard skills and insights provided by any medical school. But beyond the trust, we also hope that at some time in the not-too-distant past, our attending physician will have learned something at the hands of an undomesticated system. Heidi Baumert will be such an attending physician. When you see her reading your chart, studying lab results, interpreting X rays and scans, you will also see a look of caution on her face. Back in her memory will be the images of a pond, a bluegill, parasitic worms, and a microscope with a box of slides nearby. She will be looking at a record of some kind, but part of her mind will be focused on something that happened years earlier, when she knew, absolutely knew, that there had been a parasite on a gill, but couldn't see it in the "printout." If the only reason you've encountered her is a nasty cut that needs a few stitches, then you can rest assured that your doctor can easily forget the sunfish gills. But if it's something more serious, then you want desperately for her to remember sitting at that microscope hour after hour, knowing something had been present in her specimens, but with each passing minute questioning, more and more, the combination of technology and biology that was supposed to give her an easy answer. Was her sunfish project a failure? No. It was a rousing success. She learned a level of caution, and of healthy suspicion, that all physicians require but only an encounter with undomesticated systems can teach.

Adam decided to explore the relationships between sunfish and their gill parasites in a different manner. He chose largemouth bass, primarily because members of this species usually have heavy infections of several species. His question was also one of host specificity, but at a much smaller physical scale than Megan's. Instead of focusing on ponds and whole fish, Adam set out to determine whether the parasites sorted themselves out, by species, on the individual gill arches, on particular sections of the gill arches, and on gill filaments. A fish has eight gill arches, four to a side. Each arch has a double row of flat filaments, each shaped sort of like a spearhead with the point out (backward when they're in the fish). Each filament also has folds that function to increase the surface area over which the water flows; these folds are called lamellae. Adam decided he would fix bass gills in hot formalin, then examine each filament for worms. Those that were infected would be prepared much as Heidi had done except for the paraffin embedding, the result being a stained specimen attached to its gill filament. Each worm would be identified and several observations would be made regarding its angle and position of attachment.

With these data, Adam would eventually be able to determine whether these worms interacted with one another. He would also be able to answer another, almost philosophical, question, namely, what is a heavy infection? Two years, two bass, ten boxes of slides, 711 worms, and 3731 gill filaments later, Adam sat down to do his statistical analysis and write his paper. After another ten months, and after about fifty drafts, he finally put the thing in the mail to an international peer-reviewed journal. As is the case with Megan Collins's paper, maybe half a dozen people in the world truly care about Adam's scientific results, and of those six or seven, probably three or four care because they don't believe the paper conveys a valid picture of parasitism. That is, they have not shaken off their guiding paradigms about the way host-parasite relationships evolve. Or, they think 400+ worms on a ten-inch bass ought to constitute a heavy infection, when, in fact, there is room for 400,000 such worms.

What will Adam bring to the medical profession as a consequence of his years of struggle with an undomesticated system? First, he has learned more about the fundamental nature of infectious disease, at the hands of those two bass, than he is ever likely to learn in a medical school classroom. Second, he has lost most of his naiveté with respect to research. He knows that original investigation is difficult, time-consuming, and often likely to show you something you didn't anticipate. Third, he has learned how to take a massive data set, containing volumes of code, and mold it into a document that just about any well-educated person can read. Finally, and most important, he has learned that nobody has a monopoly on paradigms. His data showed that neither of the two prevailing (and competing) ideas about what determines the distribution of parasites on fish gills—interspecific competition and mate selection—are adequate explanations for his results. Instead, the worms distributed themselves more or less randomly. An undergraduate at a midwestern public university can challenge our perceptions of the most common way of life, albeit the model is made of fish and worms. If nobody has a monopoly on ideas surrounding the study of small-scale monogenean ecology, then nobody has a monopoly on the ideas surrounding the treatment of cancer.

My dream is that eventually such a student will combine the philosophical aspects of his undergraduate research experience with the empirical, and then extrapolate the results to a broader question. Instead of asking whether our picture of microscopic worms on sunfish gills is accurate, Adam will eventually ask whether our citizen-level view of public health is also an accurate one. That view currently seems to be missing our most dangerous hazards, namely the automobile, environmental deterioration, and political instability in far-off lands. We seem to worry most about those things that in theory we can control—smoking, alcohol consumption, measles—although certainly environmental deterioration and political instability ought to also be somewhat under our control. One of our most devastating afflictions—drug abuse—is still considered more of a crime than a disease and treated accordingly. Globally, the cultural constraints that prevent political leaders from being practical and honest with respect to AIDS prevention is a horrid tragedy that can be blamed on ego, self-deception, arrogance, and stupidity—all quite human traits. And only in 2001 did we wake up to what history has been telling us for centuries, namely that religious totalitarianism is a profound public health hazard. Some day Adam will be a teacher in addition to being a doctor. Every day he will go into the classroom or teaching clinic and face bright young people who have never encountered an undomesticated system. But every day these young people will benefit from the fact that Adam did, primarily because he will never forget what it took to extract a small piece of information from that system and bring his study to closure.

How does a teacher find, and use, an undomesticated system appropriate for an introductory biology class of 200+ students? In other words, how do we export this aspect of field parasitology back to the city? I suggest we begin by remembering that what many of us perceive to be a problem—namely—the inability to manipulate a particular system, is not a problem at all. In fact, this so-called "problem" is actually a pedagogical strength of our teaching materials. We know that the struggle is far more educational than the result. This knowledge is so ancient, so deeply embedded in our idealism, that we have simply forgotten that it is also a fundamental rule of our business. The goal is not the product or the right answer; the goal is the discipline, the insight, the nonquantifiable elements we simple call "experience" that are all learned at the hands (or fins) of an undomesticated system. In the final analysis, it is far more important that we teach the human attributes—the behaviors that only human beings can bring to bear on a task—than the specific skills, technologies, or information. And in the final analysis, there is no easier way to teach these attributes than to give our students some really wild plants or animals.

How do we accomplish this task back on city campus? "Cunning" and "diabolical" are probably too strong as descriptors for, but they do convey the spirit of, a teacher's answer to this question. In the case of most university campuses, landscape vegetation is the most accessible undomesticated system for a student in a large-enrollment lecture course. No student has control over campus landscape plantings. The plants themselves may be highly domesticated strains, varieties, or species, and placed according to some well-conceived plan, but students have neither the time nor the resources to manipulate them. An experiment with oak trees is as much of a logistical impossibility for college students as an experimental infection with sunfish gill parasites would have been for Megan or Adam. Every campus has its oak tree equivalents, in abundance. All you have to do is figure out what to do with this material—that is—you must simply design an activity, then pay for it with points, that will accomplish the desired encounter between human and some small part of nature. Admittedly, the idealism is vulnerable to some kinds of student behavior. But on the positive side, the educational quality of whatever activity you inflict on your charges is directly related to the level of their honest and receptive participation, and at least some of them know it.

Chapter 5 mentioned a series of papers on campus vegetation, along with the unexpected result of discovering students' favorite plant among several years' worth of student writing. Although it might seem like something of a letdown to go from a discussion of "cunning" and "diabolical" assignments with undomesticated systems to a flower garden, the fact remains that only the groundspeople have any control whatsoever over campus plantings. So neither students nor faculty can do much about their local landscape except study it, think about it, devise ways to use it without consuming it, and talk about it as immediately available, albeit contrived, wilderness. I suspect that if I could play go-around-the-room (see Chapter 4) with thirty of my fellow faculty members from various departments, the topic being "How might one make use of campus landscape vegetation in teaching?" the answers would be a small but stunning book about instructional resources.

My colleagues would never put up with such an exercise, however, and certainly not with me as the instigator. They are too proud, too strangled by their paradigms, too worried about their research, and too embarrassed to admit being unable to think of an idea. One might be much more successful with a mixture of freshman honors students, soda pop and cookies, and an hour to "waste." From having combined such ingredients many times in the past, I can imagine the results. Although the following words did not *actually* come directly from any young people such as Michelle Novak who you met in the opening pages of this book, they did come indirectly because their basic ideas were contained in various papers among the thousands I have read.

> "Use tracks in the snow to figure out how the squirrels use various trees."
>
> "Find every sign of illness or insect damage on every plant and speculate on why some plants are healthy and others are not. Do this for both different species and different individuals of the same species."
>
> "Make up really stupid common names for plants, put these names on the labels, and see if anyone notices."
>
> "Put some really obscene common names on these plants, *then* see if anyone actually reads the labels!"
>
> "Make up a love story between two flowers. Better yet, make up two different kinds of love stories, depending on whether the plants are monecious or dioecious."

Do all these suggestions sound immature and useless? To the uninitiated, they might. But one day I asked a group of students to walk out on campus and "have an intense botanical experience." After all, most biologists feel very strongly about whatever parts of nature they study. Many of us, for example, have had "intense entomological experiences," or "intense avian experiences." Why not ask students to do the same thing, sort of play biologist for a few short hours, and complete the circle of what it means to construct a personal identify from your study of nature? There is no compelling reason whatsoever not to ask students to do what teachers do. So I did. What follows is one (untitled) result, used here with permission of the student who wrote it, but who asked that her name not be revealed. You can judge for yourself whether the assignment worked.

I once had a relationship with an ex-boyfriend that I could classify as an intense botanical experience. Our relationship consisted of numerous serious conversations, and whenever we had something serious to discuss, we seemed to find a need to discuss it in some botanical setting. The most common settings of these conversations were the Sunken Gardens or any gazebo on East Campus. Many of our conversations were unpleasant, but discussing our conflicts in these natural, botanical settings somehow made our problems seem less devastating or threatening. The natural beauty of the flowers, trees, and foliage made our disagreements seem insignificant in the vast wonder of nature. They also provided a good distraction when we did not want to look at each other, or when we were trying to think of the right words to express how we felt.

I remember sitting in a wooden gazebo on East Campus, staring at the leafy green vines that intertwined the columns of the gazebo, trying to figure out how they happened to grow like that so simply, yet so complicatedly. I related the tangled vines to my problems with my boyfriend, which had grown so complicated that I felt we would never be able to unravel them. Yet I also remember walking through the Sunken Gardens hand-in-hand, though feeling the distance between us. However, admiring the beauty in the paths of brightly colored flowers made me feel like our problems were insignificant in the grand scheme of things and could be worked out.

Whenever we would have a fight or major disagreement, my room turned into an intense botanical experience because of all the flowers he sent me when he knew he had acted wrongly. The fragrance of the room could be overwhelming with the scents of carnations, mixed floral arrangements, flowers picked from the garden, or red roses, depending on how badly he had messed up.

This may seem like a paper meant more for an English class than for a biology class, however, my most intense botanical experiences can be related to some emotion or emotional experience. The relationship eventually ended in an East Campus gazebo surrounded by foliage and pine trees. I felt hidden from anyone or anything outside of that gazebo. I felt trapped, yet I knew I would soon be set free.

I have not generalized my negative experiences as hostility or dislike for nature or gardens. However, strolling through East Campus or the Sunken Gardens does stir up some buried emotions and sickening feelings. Yet nature does not symbolize unhappiness or heartache for me. When I study a flower and recognize its pleasant scent and intricate markings, I cannot help but wonder how it turned out so perfectly, despite everything that could happen to damage its natural and fragile state. It seems to have a hidden inner strength. I am also filled with a sense of hope when I see the same flowers grow back year after year, sometimes appearing more beautiful and stronger than ever. To me, nature symbolizes the hope in new beginnings and the reality in growing stronger and improving oneself through each new experience. I hope that my future botanical experiences will be somewhat more pleasant, yet I believe there always lies a lesson to be learned in nature.

Did this individual encounter an undomesticated system? Regardless of the fact that all of these settings—the Sunken Gardens, the gazebos placed around our agricultural campus—are highly contrived, built primarily of cultivars, for her the plants were as wild as if they'd been out in a local creek bed. Did she test any hypotheses, do any experiments, perform any statistical analyses, look up anything on the Web, use any on-line databases to find out how gazebos should be designed and which species were most appropriate for Sunken Gardens, in order to write this full-credit paper? No. Did she have a valid educational experience with living organisms? According to her paper, the answer must be yes. Will her "intense botanical experience" stick with her to the same extent Megan's, Adam's, or Heidi's intense parasitological experiences will stick with them? Again, if the paper is any indication, the answer must be yes. Could she test a hypothesis, look up something on the Web, and find out which species were most appropriate for Sunken Gardens? Sure. But if that had been what I'd asked for, you would not be reading this paper. And if that had been the assignment, I would never have learned—almost by accident—how to bring the Eden experience home to the city.

10

DEATH AND RESURRECTION

*If it were not for the constant renewal and replacement going on before your eyes,
the whole place would turn to stone and sand under your feet.*
—Lewis Thomas (from *Lives of a Cell*)

At the time he wrote the essays, originally published in the *New England Journal of Medicine*, which eventually became his book *Lives of a Cell*, Lewis Thomas was an acclaimed cancer researcher and president of Sloan-Kettering Cancer Center in New York. Among his twenty-nine chapters, the one entitled "Death in the Open" seems to resonate most strongly with the younger undergrads I have in introductory courses. From reading many of their papers and excuses for missing exams, it seems that death, usually of a grandparent but often, sadly, of a former high-school classmate, figures prominently in their emotional lives. I get the distinct impression from their papers that something previously hidden suddenly has been revealed: an abstraction has now been given substance. For students at any biological field program, "Death in the Open" is particularly relevant, because Thomas begins his essay with a discussion of roadkill, one of our prime sources of teaching material: "Seen from a car window they appear as fragments, evoking memories of woodchucks, skunks . . . etc." Thomas eventually addresses death as a natural phenomenon, and ends with a comment on humanity: "Less than half a century from now, our replacements will have more than doubled the numbers. It is hard to see how we can continue to keep the secret, with such multitudes doing the dying." The secret he is talking about is that of the death of our fellow human beings, a truly "vast mortality" of some 50 million a year.

Czeslaw Milosz, a Polish Nobel Prize winner for literature, also deals with death in a way that is both historical and personal. Milosz (2001) comments that not only "has [death] made an especially spectacular appearance in my century," in his case the twentieth, but also that "it is the real heroine of the literature and art which is contemporary with my lifetime." He is certainly correct about the literature and art, and especially so if television and film can be considered literature and art, which I assert they can, although probably not in the way Milosz was thinking when he wrote those words. The United States is probably singular among modern superpowers in its propensity for public moralistic debate, although little of this discourse has truly noble underpinnings. No, the argument is over the never-ending parade of mayhem and murder that passes for entertainment.

The participants in this public discussion are those who see a causal link between film and behavior, and who are either unable or unwilling to disassociate sex from violence, typically for religious reasons, versus those who value freedom of expression over responsibility for content. The latter group includes those who see virtually any content as legitimate material for literary and artistic expression, and who, naturally, view the former group as repressive. Neither side will ever win this debate. Unless the twenty-first century is quite different from the twentieth, some time early in the twenty-second century, a literary successor to Milosz will be able to repeat his evaluation of the previous hundred years. Television, motion pictures, and the daily news will continue to reflect one another in their depiction of carnage, essentially intermingling fact and fiction. This is the cultural environment into which I lead students to kill insects and fish, then videotape the results so that I can give a practical exam on the "material."

Whenever I develop an undergraduate laboratory exercise that involves death of an animal, even a beetle or an earthworm, both Thomas's and Milosz's words come back to me, along with those of E. O. Wilson (1978, *On Human Nature*) and Paul Fussell (1989, *Wartime*). In his chapter on aggression, Wilson talks about the dehumanization of fellow humans as a prelude to violence, especially in times of social conflict. Fussell is more explicit, using WWII as an example, and citing various ways in which we dehumanized our enemies through the use of names, thus desensitizing not only our soldiers, but also citizens back home. Thus from reading these works, I've become at least somewhat sensitized to the words that accompany killing. In parasitology class we routinely sacrifice animals in order to discover "who's infected with whom," the basic observations necessary to ana-lyze any parasitic relationship, but I've never felt it necessary to call a channel catfish some demeaning name in order to either hasten or validate its demise. If the channel catfish happens to be a large one, then it can also be a fairly dangerous animal because of its spines and strength, so killing it is no trivial task. This fact alone tends to quiet people down, lending a degree of soberness to the occasion, and I get personally involved in the act primarily because of safety issues.

The first time students are asked to do their own killing, however, their reactions are characteristically divided along gender lines, espe-cially if we're working on smaller vertebrates such as sunfish or toads. The men are most concerned about having scissors sturdy enough to cut through a backbone. The women typically want a thoroughly dead and nontwitching specimen delivered to their dissecting pans. Inevitably I have to remind some students to dispatch their animals quickly, without fanfare. The *fact* of cutting off a fish's head is not what concerns me in this instance; it's the *words* that accompany the act. These words reveal much about our deep view of nonhuman species, especially in a local society that values fishing and hunting both as cultural birthrights and as economic engines. To someone in search of microscopic worms hanging off a gill filament, killing a four-inch long wild animal is not confirmation of one's manhood. Without belaboring the point, when we've come to Cedar Point to study parasites, cutting the head off a fish is not only a prerequisite to such study, it's also all that it is.

After five weeks of dissection, I usually end the summer session with an extended discussion of the Thomas, Wilson, and Fussell books, as well as some more modern cases involving massive human destruction in Rwanda, Kosovo, and the Persian Gulf War (see Power, 2002). There is a simple reason why I often feel that such a discussion is necessary: When you come to know an insect, snail, or "minnow" rather intimately, and build your academic identity on the scientific study of their parasites, then it is not so easy to objectify these lowly creatures. The organisms with which you do your first real research project, showing your professor you are truly capable of conducting an original scientific investigation and earning your guaranteed-get-in letter of recommendation to medical school, suddenly become valuable to you. They are no longer worthless trash, they are no longer repulsive, and most important, they are no longer unknowns, but instead they have become a part of your emotional and intellectual library. They've given their lives, yes, but they've also given you the irreplaceable power of experience, and the intellectual sophistication that comes from doing research that you would never have been given, had you not set about to study their parasites.

Not long after beginning the Field Parasitology course, I started looking for host-parasite systems that did not involve endangered species, for which collecting permits could be obtained with only routine paperwork, and which were decidedly nonhuman—that is—not furry and warm with large eyes. Additionally, these organisms needed to be available in fairly large numbers in order to serve as training exercises in public-health-type statistics as well as in parasitology. For most premed students, a quantitative exercise on parasite populations and communities would be the first, and perhaps the only, original experience they would have with the distribution of infectious agents in a population until they got into practice and had to deal with an epidemic. And if, as "health-care professionals," they found themselves caught up in a military adventure, then suddenly they would likely be wishing they'd studied the biology of infectious organisms over and over again, instead of being so enamored of reproductive physiology, cancer, and cardiovascular function. So because of my determination to keep the public-health-statistics component of my courses a real experience, we quantify as much as we can. In the process, we certainly kill a lot of small animals—damselflies, mosquitoes, beetles, snails, fish, toads.

By way of comparison to the killing of wild animals in Eden, about 32,000 Americans die each year of gunshot wounds. Another 42,000 die in automobile accidents. From a biologist's perspective, especially a biologist who studies small organisms, the clearing of tropical forests at the rate of 50–100 acres *a minute* for the past several decades, results in the death of uncountable, but truly beautiful and wondrous, organisms. Automobile drivers hit 14,000 deer in Iowa during a recent year, at a cost of about $3,000 per incident ($42 million a year in damage, not including injuries to people). A friend of mine who regularly rode a bicycle along a country highway and counted roadkill, then extrapolated that sample to the national level, estimated that at any moment there would be 75 million birds lying dead on America's highways. I read a report (unconfirmed) that housecats in Great Britain killed an estimated 60 million songbirds a year. The arch monument over Interstate 80 near Kearney, Nebraska, has cost one human life, and not too many years ago the *Omaha World-Herald* reported that the increase in speed limits from 55 MPH to 65 MPH on I-80 resulted in approximately one additional human life a month. The speed limit is now 75 MPH. A trip through any packing plant makes your hamburger and bacon look quite different from the actual animals they once were. In addition to all this death, we have the issue of quality of life for those still living who, for various reasons, do not have access to the humanizing influences of quality education, a safe place to sleep at night, adequate health care, and meaningful employment. Into this latter category fall millions of Americans and billions of other human beings around the world.

I'm not condemning anyone for contributing to the foregoing figures. I am, however, simply stating the obvious: that just by living our normal, twenty-first century human lives, we contribute to the death of uncountable numbers of organisms, and except for the ones closest to us, generally ignore the deaths of other human beings. And when massive human death seems either a political expedient or an inconvenience, we officially ignore it. Samantha Power's (2002) book, *"A Problem from Hell": America and the Age of Genocide,* validates that last claim in sobering fashion, beginning with the Armenians on April 25, 1915, and finishing with the Kurds and Kosovo Albanians in the 1980s and '90s. On a more personal level, few people read the newspaper obituaries in a large city, then bemoan all of those who have passed away, every day. No matter how much tragedy, how much sorrow, is actually found between the lines of those obit items, the rest of us usually flip past that page quickly on the way to sports and/or comics.

Thus it does not bother me very much to use small animals in order to provide young people, many of whom will become physicians, with their first scientific experience involving infectious organisms (we all have nonscientific experiences with infectious organisms). I do appreciate the fact, however, that an intimate encounter with death, as when someone cuts the head off an insect, can produce an emotional reaction. In this particular case, we have chosen to terminate a life in order to study something that most people find repulsive (a parasite), even though that repulsive organism is living the most common way of life on earth. I only ask that students remember their parasitology when their kid comes home from day care with lice or pinworms and they wonder how to cure the infection (it's not terribly difficult, at least in the case of pinworms, although everyone in the family has to take the antihelminthic.)

I also encourage students to undertake a personal examination of their own reasons for reacting as they do to the welfare of other organisms, as part of their overall education as biological science majors. From a teacher's perspective, it doesn't matter much whether the other animals involved in this introspection are insects or fellow humans. I'm guessing that the closer an organism is to us personally, or the closer in appearance and demeanor to humans in general, or the younger the organism, then the stronger will be our reaction to its death. This principle figures prominently in politics and government regulation surrounding the use of animals in research and teaching, as well as the most persistent political issue of modern times, namely, abortion. Thus the death of a baby cocker spaniel has an infinitely higher emotional content than the death of a mosquito or cockroach, at least to the average person. And if we contribute to the deaths, then that of the puppy will probably linger in our minds for a lifetime, whereas the mosquito and cockroach will be forgotten as soon as we get over the pleasure, and probably smug satisfaction, of having killed them.

None of my students have ever commented on the killing of a plant. Yet in the Biodiversity course, where we use geraniums and snapdragons twice a semester, students often ask if they can take the plants home. In this request I detect a subtle emotional attachment to the specimens they have used in order to learn something of nature. I never know what happens to these adopted lab plants. Of the ones I've personally kept, the snaps always die fairly quickly, but the geraniums get leggy and sprawling in my north-facing office window. I have this vision of my students becoming seriously attached to these plants, succumbing to the same principle that applies to their research animals. In my mind, former Biodiversity students now have geraniums in their Omaha apartments, or maybe have given their mothers cuttings. Thus the germ line of a single *Pelargonium domesticum*, started in the biotech greenhouse for use in a freshman class, is now established in a flowerbed out in North Platte, Nebraska.

In this imaginary scenario, whenever these students water their plants, they get a whiff of the distinctive geranium oils, and it reminds them of their younger, freer, premed school days. I know that when I water the one I keep in my lab, the smell reminds me of what I did to write the plant dissection and identification exercises. I went out into my own yard and dug up a geranium. Then I took it into my basement, did a careful dissection, studied the flowers and their parts under a microscope, and made extensive drawings and notes. These original pages were then photocopied and put into the set of lab exercises as a lesson on how to be an old-time naturalist. Around the world, uncountable, and probably astronomical, numbers of geranium plants have been started and have died during the time I have been teaching Biodiversity. But one gave its life so that hundreds of students would have this example of how to study geraniums, and by extension other plants, and how to record their observations. That single plant has achieved a certain kind of immortality. It's not been resurrected literally, of course, but certainly symbolically. The same could be said for every individual plant used as a model for any artist for any purpose and now immortalized in works ranging from Cézanne still lifes to the engravings found in medieval herbals. They've all died in the process of study, then been resurrected as platonic archetypes that, in turn, shape our expectations of what their species should be like. Unless we routinely go to the field for some hands-on encounters with vegetation, the art eventually fulfills not only our expectations of nature, but also, presumably, then our actions toward nature.

As for an original encounter with vegetation, however, I know that in the case of my lab manual drawing, the very act of studying this single plant, and particularly the way I did that study—alone with only a pencil, paper, microscope, and a razor blade—completely altered my view of geraniums. Ideally, a similar altered view inspires my students to take their plants home after lab. Thus my own experience as a teacher mimics my hopes for the students that also approach their plants with only the simple tools of the naturalist's trade—pencil, paper, blade, lens, and interest. The knowledge about plants, or about anything that we actually kill during a laboratory exercise, is always secondary to the real objective, which is the incorporation of our experience with the one into our attitude about the many. I have seen this assimilation happen often enough to know that young people are quite capable of achieving it, at least when the victims are minnows or damselflies. What I don't see happening at all is the deaths of grandmothers shaping a nation's attitudes about the deaths of fathers and brothers who happen to live in nations we consider political enemies. This disconnect is the great failing of biology the profession. The belief that this disconnect is none of our business is one great failing of American academia.

As described earlier, periodically I send students to the University of Nebraska State Museum (UNSM) to do various writing exercises. UNSM, located in a building named Morrill Hall, is one of the nation's truly fine university museums. Its centerpiece is Elephant Hall, a gigantic room inhabited by skeletons of proboscidians that roamed the Great Plains at various times over the past 50 million years— titanotheres, mastodonts, and, of course, several species of mammoths. Nebraska is the heart of mammoth country, and in Elephant Hall one can find a record of their giant molars from virtually every one of the state's ninety-three counties. I have one of these teeth sitting on my desk at the university, a gift from a former student who uncovered several on his family farm. An 18-foot tall, fully articulated skeleton of *Mammuthus (Archidiskodon) imperator maibeni*, known locally and affectionately as Archie, the world's largest wooly mammoth specimen, stands along the east side of Elephant Hall. And all across the south end of this cathedrallike room is a truly stunning mural, painted by a young artist named Marc Marcuson. The scene is probably from late February or early March, 10,000 B.C. A herd of mammoths, including their young, led by a life-size Archie, is moving across a bleak prairie landscape, through a gravely streambed, toward the viewer. Their breath fogs. Sandhill cranes scatter before the herd, wings pumping, guttural calls echoing off the shallow cut banks. You can feel the wet, biting, chill wind. You can hear the mammoths' thunderous breathing, their heavy footsteps in the gravel, you can feel the ground shake, and you can smell the dirt and sodden grass.

Of course this wondrous thrill of being transported back into the Pleistocene epoch is all in your mind. Everything in Elephant Hall— from the synthetic fiber carpet to the 30-foot high domed plaster ceiling to the petrified tibias and scapulas to the pigments in Marcuson's mural—is dead as a doornail. Yet those who assembled the exhibit created something that allows another human being to acquire a certain kind of experience, which can grow, internally, eventually producing feelings, desires, and a worldview. Marc Marcuson is only the most recent of UNSM muralists. Elizabeth Dolan who preceded him by sixty years, Erwin Barbour who excavated Archie and his companions, Bertrand Schultz who raised millions for the building of Morrill Hall exhibits, Hugh Genoways who administered the latest Elephant Hall renovation, and many forgotten carpenters and electricians, together over the span of nearly a century, did something a biology teacher must do every day in class, namely take a bunch of dead stuff and make it come alive. But this problem is not unique to biology. Teachers of history, sociology, literature, philosophy must all reverse the process of death in order to bring their disciplines to life.

How do we accomplish this resurrection? I don't claim to have the final or complete answer to this question, but like every biology teacher I do have the experience of actually trying to connect student minds with the dead—preserved specimens, textbook pictures—then assessing (grading!) the results. What's discussable is the extent to which a *real* resurrection is actually necessary, versus whether student behavior can be changed by only an experience of the mind. Of course I believe the latter; every teacher must. Besides, there is simply too much evidence to support the hypothesis that an entire world can be constructed, along with its operating principles, out of only neural impulses. For starters, try the game Dungeons and Dragons, the book *Dune* and its successors, the *Star Wars* films, and the *Lord of the Rings* trilogy. Real people can easily live in their own universe, behave according to some set of concocted rules, and teach, or coerce, others to do the same. A quick check on the veracity of this claim can be made by anyone with access to a computer. If the aforementioned books, games, and films are not adequate proof, go to the Web, click on "search," type in "creation science," and hit the "go" button. Within seconds you will discover an army built on grand delusions.

If the creationists can build a planetary system from ideas alone, then so can the biologists and historians, although we have an obligation to make ours consistent with what is actually known about Earth. Nevertheless, as real as the Devonian period might be to a professor of paleontology, it's as distant as the Crab Nebula to the average undergraduate, and equally as noncompelling. So we must use some tricks to add the fourth dimension to our repertoire of pedagogical power tools. I have two such tricks that seem to work: a leaf and a fossil. The fossils that I use are extraordinarily abundant, readily accessible, and so well studied that any respectable paleontologist would consider them hackneyed symbols of boredom, sort of in the same category as earthworms or cockroaches. To an undergraduate, however, they are unusual and unexpected gifts that come from a far-off place—my secret collecting site in Oklahoma. I usually pass them out on April 22nd, or thereabouts, in celebration of Earth Day. My students hold these fossils in their hands—tangible items from 70 million years ago—while we talk about the long parade of organisms passing through their lives. That parade includes all the historical figures any of them views as a living and influential presence—from Jesus to George Washington to the plants shredded for their last night's salad.

The leaf is that of a ginkgo. My campus has rows of these trees planted along many sidewalks. Unless destroyed by humans, each ginkgo tree will stand in its place for a thousand years, longer than any modern university has stood. If only a thousand students a day, on the average, walk past a single ginkgo, and we do not purposefully destroy it, then by the time it dies, that one tree will have seen 365 million undergrads. I usually pick a ginkgo leaf and take it into the large auditorium where I teach Introductory Biology to 230 freshman every fall. That first lecture begins with the words DNA, that infamous and ubiquitous molecule we all know from the O. J. Simpson trial. By holding a ginkgo leaf, one touches genetic information that has been present on Earth for 200 million years, surviving by replication. The genes are there, intact. Any human who recognizes a ginkgo tree today could, if somehow transported back in time those 200 million years, instantly recognize that same tree. The nucleotide sequences—those familiar combinations of C, A, T, and G—that spelled "ginkgo" during the Triassic period, still spell "ginkgo" today.

What should one do with a 70-million year old oyster shell and a leaf that are more symbols of the Mesozoic Era than of the Third Millennium? Ideally one should play go-around-the-room. The question for the day would be how could you bring this specimen back to life? For the leaf, the answer is simple biotechnology, regardless of whether such technology would actually work in the lab (isolate the ginkgo cells, put them in just the right culture conditions, grow the plants from those cell, etc.). Any freshman text has enough genetic-engineering content to make such a task routine, at least in the mind of a freshman, regardless of how nonroutine or outright impossible it might be for a professional biologist. For the shell, however, answers range from the mystical (create a religion based on the shell and brainwash people to *act* as if it's alive) to the sci-fi standard (there is a living population somewhere on Earth; all we have to do is go find it).

I actually performed this "bring back to life" exercise in a more formal way one year, by sending my students to the Paleozoic gallery of the museum. They were asked to play the role of a biology professor who had just discovered large populations of living trilobites, a natural community with several different species. The assignment was to write a laboratory exercise that would use these living specimens, illustrate the properties of trilobites, and reveal their diverse behaviors, feeding habits, and development, an exercise that depended, not on the fossils, but on the living organisms. The results were disappointing, yet, I felt, strangely revealing of certain mental processes. I was never convinced I understood those processes in the way a teacher should. So I just admitted that the paper assignment was not really a scientific study of the human mind, and never discussed those results with anyone, until now.

At the time I gave this assignment—to a second-semester zoology class—the introductory biology labs of the previous semester had used commercially available pillbugs, *Porcellio scaber*, in a behavior exercise. Although extant pillbugs are tiny compared to many trilobites, they do bear a superficial resemblance to those iconographic arthropods of the ancient seas. Evidently that resemblance impressed my students as being more than superficial. Thus what I got back in the trilobite resurrection exercise was a repeat of the pillbug labs. Not a single student picked anything that was of *trilobite* importance, as opposed to *pillbug* importance, to "teach" his or her fellow students. Reading through these 200+ well-written but relatively boring and homogeneous papers, I came to four different conclusions. In the first two conclusions, I felt that my students had either simply copied their labs from a previous semester out of convenience, or were so taken with the fact that at first glance trilobites and pillbugs look similar, that they assumed they were similar. Therefore, there was nothing new or different about a trilobite that could not be discovered in three hours using a pillbug. The third conclusion was somewhat disturbing, especially for an educator: Perhaps they assumed that whatever they'd done with a pillbug the previous semester was the "correct" thing to do—necessary and sufficient for a complete understanding of any pillbuglike organism, even one that had been extinct for 240 million years.

The fourth conclusion, however, was much more philosophical and even mysterious. Perhaps, I thought, giving these nineteen- and twenty-year-olds credit for some subconscious traits, they simply assumed that when it came to arthropods, there was no distinction between life and death. Maybe something beyond undergraduate obedience to the "what I am responsible for" rules had very naturally connected their experience with living terrestrial crustaceans a few months earlier to fossil remnants of a once flourishing and diverse Paleozoic fauna. Without thinking twice about the underlying mental processes or the image that resulted, they had resurrected a long-extinct group of animals and never questioned their own ability—or willingness—to do so. I wondered whether they didn't see any difference between life and death only when the subject was arthropods. I wondered whether life and death were not really alternative states unless the subject was something in which they'd invested *emotional* energy.

On the other hand, maybe they'd inadvertently revealed a relatively powerful teaching device—namely—the assignment subtly designed to tap this tendency for resurrection. A three-hour hands-on *experience* with pillbugs had enabled their associative powers. I realize this line of thought probably extends the importance of a paper-writing experience far beyond what it should be, although when something sticks in your mind the way the pillbug-trilobite exercise does, then the importance is not zero. But thinking back on what Eden provides, the trilobite-pillbug association seems a key to a kind of teaching that we tend to forget about, at least at the university level. Instead of sending students to a museum to resurrect trilobites, we should send pillbugs home with them. Instead of asking students if they want geraniums, we should be telling them that they have to take geraniums. Instead of giving students the option of avoiding daily duty to a nonhuman species, we should be giving them responsibilities and making them vulnerable to an emotional encounter with some organisms beyond their dog, cat, or significant other. Maybe they simply need to live with some wild thing that is not necessarily cooperative or happy to be in confinement (although I suppose that could describe some significant others!).

The Folsom Children's Zoo in Lincoln, Nebraska, has rediscovered this deeply buried pedagogical treasure with a program called Zoo to You. Granted, the organisms involved are mostly cute—mice, hamsters, pigeons, guinea pigs—but some, such as mealworms, are not so cute, at least in the mind of an average person. The Zoo to You program involves taking these animals into schools and leaving them in the care of the fourth-grade students. In the classroom, these animals become the focus of observation, writing, art, behavioral data collection, and experiences shared via a Web site. Beyond all the biology, however, someone has to feed these creatures, change their litter, and take them home on weekends. Mimi Wickless, coordinator of this wonderful activity, attaches only one caveat to this weekend and vacation responsibility: "There can't be a predator in the home," she says, meaning, of course, dogs, cats, or ferrets. Parents don't count as predators; instead, they're involved in a communal way—not only with their own child's commitment to the object of study—but also, indirectly, with every other child in the class. "Commitment to the object of study" is the key phrase; all professionals who do original work, whether they be biologists, physicists, astronomers, artists, literary scholars, historians, or economists, are committed to the objects of their study. They bring these objects to life through such commitment, such possession, even though that possession might be a shared one. I challenged Mimi one day:

"Would these children have the same intellectual attachment to a rock?"

She didn't know for sure, but the smile on her face told me she was convinced it would happen.

My own father certainly had an intellectual attachment to rocks, a love that went far beyond his need to interact with them as a petroleum geologist. At the end of a long and hot summer session at Cedar Point, my students and I usually take a final field trip to the South Platte River at Roscoe, entering the river at the Thalken property, owned by one of western Nebraska's extremely generous ranchers, Charles Thalken. We walk the sand and clear shallows, reflecting on what we've accomplished in the previous five weeks, picking up feathers, beaver-chewed sticks, snails, pieces of crayfish, and simply talking to one another about these treasures in parasitological terms. As we leave the river and walk back toward the vans, I stop at a place near the fence and pick up a rock, then talk about how old-time geologists can tell a grand story of Earth using only a chunk of graphic granite as prop. I wish—publicly, in front of my students—that I had listened more to my father when he was alive. I then pick out special rocks, placing one carefully in each student's hands, with the gestures of a gift. I remind them of Charlie Thalken's generosity, and his father's generosity before that, to give us a key, both literal and metaphorical, to a classroom as rich and compelling as the South Platte River. Do these rocks come alive in student hands? I hope so. Will the gift of a single stone, picked up from an almost sacred and legendary place, stick with them for a lifetime, constantly reminding them of what they learned, how they learned it, resurrect the most wonderful learning experiences of their short lives as budding scientists? The idealist never doubts for a moment that is the case. After all, we do give diamonds, don't we, to special people?

11

BIG TALK AT THE
WHITE GATE

Great minds discuss ideas;
Average minds discuss events;
Small minds discuss people.
—Unknown author

The epigraph quote is often attributed to Hyman Rickover, although various Web sites credit Eleanor Roosevelt equally as often. The attributions are never accompanied by a reference to an original source. Both individuals may have used it, or its underlying wisdom, in speeches and writing. The quote may also be phrased as "Great men talk about ideas; mediocre men talk about things; small men talk about people." Regardless of how it's worded or who originally said or wrote it, the concept is quintessentially Rickoverian. Although remembered most for his central role in the development of the U. S. Navy nuclear submarine fleet, Rickover's idealism extended far beyond the military. He was born in Poland, in 1900, but twenty-two years later graduated from the United States Naval Academy. Somewhere along the way between his student days and his ascendancy to positions of enormous influence over U.S. military technology, he recognized the link between education, national security, and the type of freedom Americans enjoyed. He fretted enough over the fate of his adopted nation that he addressed its human-resource development problems in books, speeches, and testimony before congressional hearings.

Oliver Wendell Holmes also addressed the nature of intellect in some of his "conversations" with himself. Holmes (1891) compared people to houses, suggesting that there were one-, two-, and three-storied intellects; the latter were people who used their idealism and imagination, and received their illumination from above, through skylights. Holmes was not so disparaging of the lesser minds, however. In his metaphor, second-storied minds compared, reasoned, and generalized whereas first-floor folks collected facts. Neither second nor third stories of a house can stand up, of course, without the foundation and ground floor. The challenge in education, it seems, is to produce people who can, and will, live in their entire house, who understand the importance of spending time in every room, and who have learned how important the stairs are. The alternative to meeting this challenge is to assume that our genes have forever stuck us on one floor, a sort of biological house arrest. A real teacher reluctantly accepts this alternative; instead, he or she constantly strives to lead students up and down the stairs as necessary, talking to one another all the way.

It is virtually impossible to argue with the assertion that great minds discuss ideas, although in all honesty, talk about other people is often the most fascinating of the three general topic areas. This observation explains why English and history courses are, or at least can easily be made into, rather compelling classroom experiences and why philosophy courses can seem both magnificent and threatening at the same time. In English and philosophy, the ideas are easily and inevitably associated with people and their particular struggles. Where does that leave biology? No matter which version of the quote you prefer, biology is left right in the middle. Science, and consequently science talk, deals mostly with things and events; we scientists are notorious for comparing them in an attempt to discover generalities. Our folk heroes—for example, Charles Darwin and Albert Einstein—are the few who transcend our preoccupation with things and take the next step, assembling grand and overarching ideas from their observations.

In *Lives of a Cell*, his best-selling book from the mid-70s, Lewis Thomas addresses the issue of communication in essay after essay. The "talk" in this case is between ants, between cells of our body, between human beings, and all kinds of other biological entities. The "language" takes equally diverse forms such as pheromones, other types of molecules, behaviors, sounds, and words. Thomas also makes the case for highly specific messages (pheromones); for messages that cause us to react in ways that are damaging to ourselves (lipopolysaccharide endotoxin); and for messages that seem to say nothing more than "I'm here," such information somehow reassuring everyone that a group is intact and functioning properly. The vast bulk of social animal "conversation" seems to be the latter. We humans are too, as we all know, highly social animals (see Wilson, 1978). So it should come as no surprise that so much of our conversation seems to function primarily to let us know that society is simply conducting business as usual. We buy groceries, get our cars fixed, go on dates, watch TV, have babies, get married and divorced, eat out, go shopping, send birthday gifts, and mow the lawn. So long as everyone does these activities, society as a whole appears to be intact. The small talk assures us everything is okay. I suspect this is why so much of our talk is about mundane subjects, whether or not everything is okay.

On the other hand, regardless of the fundamental nature of our discipline, we as teachers would obviously like to produce some great minds. Thus we must turn the conversation toward ideas—get beyond the "I'm here and buying groceries" stage. In pursuit of this goal, I submit that teachers need to remember four things about talk. First, we are in the word and symbol business, and talk is nothing more than traffic in words and symbols. Second, we have the responsibility of eliminating Small Talk and replacing it with Big Talk, or better yet, producing people who know the difference and purposefully opt for the latter at least part of the time. Admittedly, elimination of Small Talk seems like a quixotic mission impossible, and I don't believe anyone thinks it can be eliminated it altogether. After all, we need to be assured everything is okay if it actually is. But there are those times when you honestly believe well-educated, powerful, and responsible people ought to have their minds focused on something other than golf or college football. Third, if you listen closely to what people around you are saying, you'll discover quickly that Lewis Thomas is pretty much right—most of our conversation is babble, functioning primarily to convey information contained in the simple declarative sentence "I'm here." Finally, I'm convinced that in a room full of people, one person can alter the entire character of discussion just by uttering the right words. Given these four principles, any teacher ought to be able to change the world into a better place just by applying them in and outside the classroom.

What is it about our western Nebraska Eden that produces Big Talk? The answer is several things, but foremost among them is the White Gate at the entrance. During one administrative changeover, Big Talk was evidently deemed so dangerous that Cedar Point's director decided to paint the White Gate a different color. Instead, it got painted with a new coat of white. Apparently it dawned on this individual in his first administrative job that he could paint it black and students would still call it the White Gate, although safety also had something to do with the decision. When you put up a heavy steel barricade across a gravel road in western Nebraska, you'd better paint it bright white so it will catch a pickup's headlights a long way off. Most nights at the field station, students and some faculty members gather outside the White Gate to talk and watch the stars. This gate is the boundary between university property and a sort of no-man's land probably owned by an irrigation district or the Corps of Engineers but of virtually no use except as a dumping place for construction rubble. Getting off-site—away from the university if only a few feet—seems to have a releasing effect on communication. Outside the White Gate it's also possible to drink a beer although it's not really clear that such consumption is legal there, even in no-man's land. It is clear that beer is not permitted on state property inside the White Gate. The two words, "not permitted," represent a larger and somewhat abstract authority that ends precisely at the Gate. But even if beer were permitted inside, students would very likely go outside.

This short description of a social phenomenon is intended as a parable. It's the break with, or perhaps release from, authority, no matter how symbolic, that stimulates Big Talk outside the White Gate. The teacher's job, of course, then becomes that of producing a metaphorical White Gate and leading his or her students through it. Alternatively, perhaps the teacher's first task is to recognize that he or she *represents* the authority that must be defied or traversed. What is the most common and familiar manifestation of that authority? Obviously in the classroom it's the right to speak, given first, and often always, to the teacher. As the game is played in universities, whatever comes out of a teacher's mouth is automatically considered Big Talk, at least for exam purposes. Such Big Talk may be later deflated in dorm rooms, but at the time it's uttered it establishes authority. In the classroom, the right to speak, and the content of this speech, is further constrained by the list of appropriate questions and comments, as well as the paralanguage commentary that is part of every school experience at all levels.

Academic paralanguage includes attitude, tone of voice, posture, respect for the furniture, clothing, newspapers, cell phones, pagers, headsets, and even whispered conversations with neighbors. Yes, all of these subtle—and at times not so subtle—forms of communication are seen regularly in university classrooms across the country, and especially in the large, introductory course multimedia auditoriums. When a student takes, or makes, a cell-phone call in the middle of a lecture on genetics, then that student might as well have told the teacher directly that his or her version of Big Talk is total bullshit. When a professor lets a student read a newspaper in class, that professor is telling his students that whatever they are doing in that room is not very important to him, implying there is no reason why it should be important to them, and, in fact, that the teacher is talking Small Talk. The newspaper and cell phone represent assumptions of authority; that's why I tend to tell people to either put them away or leave when I see them being used out in the audience. Such an exchange does not result in my students being led through a White Gate; more often than not, when I have to ask a couple of lovebirds discussing their wedding in the thirty-seventh row to shut up or leave, the gate is slammed shut for everyone. From such experiences come my strong belief that students themselves have far more control over the quality of their own institutions than do either the faculty or the administrators.

There is probably a massive psychological literature on various forms of authority, but this book is not the place to get too sober about that subject. Instead, I'll point out some of the most obvious ones, then discuss various methods for stepping outside the White Gate, no matter where it's located. The authority forms we deal with every day in university settings include institutional grading systems, faculty testing and grading practices, any syllabus, textbooks, lists of graduation requirements, standards of beauty, athletic traditions, class schedules, and whatever students have been taught during their first eighteen years by relatives, siblings, schools, and religious institutions. All of these factors can be quite intimidating and oppressive, especially when faculty members use or submit to any or all of them, even in subtle or subconscious ways.

Any elimination, by a faculty member, of the authoritarian content of our typical business accoutrements is a step outside the White Gate. The most vulnerable of these accoutrements, and the one over which faculty members have total control, is their own grading system. That's why I look continually for ways to subvert my own system, which is at least in part controlled by the authority of both my institution and my profession. In other words, I must be able to defend whatever I enter on a grade roster at the end of the semester. The defense requirement results from both professional ethics and liability. The teacher profession itself maintains its integrity only if we grade fairly and evenly, and at the university level, capriciousness often ends up being formally appealed—that is—if the grade awarded turns out to be too low in the eyes of a student. For all these reasons, work done by young people in response to the words I write on the blackboard and utter in front of class must be convertible into numbers.

This link between words and numbers is quite vulnerable to subversion, however, and indeed much of a teacher's power lies almost solely in his or her ability, or perhaps willingness, to subvert the system. Remember that what we want to accomplish is Big Talk, about ideas, instead of about football. Or, to generalize, maybe we are looking for words about ideas instead of about worldly concerns such as health, agriculture, money, politics, the military, sex, sports, and organized religion. The task, then, is to find a way to accomplish the Small Talk-to-Big Talk conversion, then evenhandedly—in fact by means of an intellectual contract between teacher and students—express that conversion into numbers that "the system" understands. The student whose work you read in Chapter 5—Billie Jean Winsett—again provides an excellent example of how this task might be accomplished. Her name came up recently in a conversation that on the surface seems almost eerily contrived, but in retrospect almost equally preordained. The conversation was with another of Ms. Winsett's teachers, a man whose classroom was a volleyball court.

My wife and I had received an invitation to a rather unusual event. Naturally, we accepted. Thus on a bitter cold, late December evening, we parked beneath a viaduct in the dark, deserted, warehouse district of our city, then walked carefully across snow-dusted bricks to a building entrance. Inside a barren atrium, we took an elevator to a third-floor loft, where we were greeted by Judy and Larry Roots, attorney and artist, respectively. Inside, an elegantly dressed woman took our coats, handed us a catalog, and pointed us toward the wine and shrimp. A flute and classical guitar duo played softly from a darkened corner. Giant panels, made of canvas and pipe, divided the large room into long sections, and also served as walls to display Larry's work of the past year. Forty abstract pieces, most of them 6 feet tall, bearing names such as *Causation Srs. No. 27*, stared down at the growing crowd. We were fans; every guest bought Larry's paintings when he was "on the way up." A friend remarked that "there are now a lot more zeros than there used to be" in the prices. I noticed a person I'd not seen in several years contemplating *18 Simultaneous Moments* (48 × 96). I greeted the man, Terry Pettit, one of the most successful university volleyball coaches in the history of the game. The last time we talked, he'd just won a national championship. We reminisced about former students we had in common. At this artsy in-crowd event surrounded by abstractions, Billie Jean Winsett's name came up naturally. For Terry, she was a dominating all-American hitter; for me, she produced the epitome of Big Talk.

"She was the most determined individual I've ever known," Terry recalled. "Even in drills, she wouldn't yield her place on the floor until she'd perfected whatever we were working on."

"She wrote four papers in my class," I said; "two of those I think about every day." Thirty-six years in the college professor business, and I think daily about two of the nearly 30,000 student papers I've read in that time? Terry Pettit's wife was suddenly curious. By the look on her face, I could tell she was wondering what this gifted athlete on a national championship team might have written so that the words would stick forever in the mind of a teacher. "*The Light Not on the Horizon*," I answered her unasked question. "It was about how a snail shell might have been the inspiration for Barnett Newman's *Horizon Light*."

At the time Billie Jean wrote this paper, the Newman painting was hanging in the Sheldon Memorial Art Gallery on our campus. I'd issued her a marine snail shell at the beginning of a semester, and along with 200 others, she'd written four papers on her individual specimen. The last of these paper assignments required that the students go to the Sheldon, pick a painting, then explain how their shell could have been the inspiration for this painting. This kind of assignment is a perfect example of one that can be done "correctly" in as many ways as there are humans on the planet. Billie Jean chose to play the role of Barnett Newman, a towering figure in the quintessentially American Abstract Expressionist movement, claiming, for the purpose of fulfilling an assignment in a zoology course, that "inspiration came from a natural masterpiece." Here is that paper. As in Chapter 5, I resisted the inclination to edit, and instead looked for the Big Talk.

The Light Not in the Horizon

Billie Jean Winsett

Walking in the midst of the hundreds of paintings an art gallery holds, an amateur might marvel at the creativity of the artist. What type of gift are they given that enables them to conjure a novel of thoughts and compact them onto a few feet of canvas? [What form of mosaic mind do they possess that allows them to place the pieces into a puzzle whereas the amateurs understand only by reducing the puzzle to pieces?] Yet we artists know that our minds do not evoke our compositions—it is our eyes that behold the depictions. Our eyes inspect the colors of the seasons, the patterns of foliage, the lighting and shading of the sun—the artwork of nature, the creator of artists' creations.

When I, Barnett Newman, painted *Horizon Light* in 1949, my mind did not conceive the painting. The inspiration, like all artistic inspiration, came from a natural masterpiece—a work of science so simple yet so intricate that no human will ever equal. This masterpiece was a tiny shell. *Horizon Light* is a 3 ft × 6 ft oil on canvas. A dark rust color engulfs a three-inch horizontal pale-blue strip that pierces through the middle. This provides for several viewpoints of a gastropod, portraying its size from a minute creature to a massive creation.

The first viewpoint I'll address is the viewpoint many people do not see. I was flying my airplane when I looked below to see the red clay protecting a silent river. The area was sparsely populated, no one was caring for the river or caring about the river. The water was its own community, a world uncaring about the land kissing it. The water world was not harming outsiders by ignoring them; they were crystal blue and self-sufficient. Yet the creatures of the land were bleeding their clay blood into its neighboring world by ignoring it. The trash and pollution they tossed to the blue beyond was the sacrifice of selfishness, suffocating self-sufficiency. As I gazed upon this image from my airplane, I hoped the human terrestrial world could become more like the seemingly insignificant snail. The snail peacefully moves from world to world, caring for each, disturbing none.

Then I focused on the snail itself. The white continuous ring on the snail was not perfectly straight, and it had numerous color inflections and impurities. Still, the snail proudly wore its shell for others to gaze upon. Nothing in nature is perfect; imperfections are the norm. Yet the nonhuman world—the water world—seems not to care. They are still united, still undenying. Thus I designed the blue stripe of *Horizon Light* so that it is not perfectly straight. It has imperfections. If everyone and everything in both worlds have imperfections, then why are humans so concerned about the flaws in their outer appearance? [Imperfection does not imply impurity. Impurity is introduced by the way one reacts to imperfection.]

Roughness is protection. The shell is not smooth, for it has small projections. These projections are not sharp enough to ward off friends, but tough enough to distract enemies. This engulfs the shell into a small circle of security. Humans need this sense of roughness. People should display their rough texture as they argue for their rights and convictions. Yet they should not be piercing, whereas they might puncture a friendship that will never return. I painted *Horizon Light* on canvas so that a rough texture would be evident. Like the snail, this rough texture can be touched but not tattered. It can be approached but not agitated.

The last viewpoint from the snail is one the snail actually sees. The snail can only see a small portion of the horizon's light as it peers out of its aperture. A thin line of blue glorifies the world in which the snail lives. The rest of the snail lives in darkness. Humans, too, only see the thin line of blue happiness. Yet this is a mental handicap, not a physical impediment. Humans refuse to see the dirty rust with which they are replacing the pure blue. Soon, the horizon will be painted with a rust blood stain. Then the mental handicap will become, analogous with the snail, a physical handicap. The cleanliness and coolness of life will be replaced with the hot, dingy, and smoky colors of brown and rust.

Horizon Light was inspired by a small shell that lives an insignificant yet pure life. The rust and corrosion of the coinciding yet contrasting world is compressing the pure blue of the world, the natural world. Then the horizon light will not be seen by the human-natural world, or the terrestrial-water world. The light will not be seen at all, unless humans become like the snail—insignificant yet pure, not significant yet unpure.

There are two sentences in brackets above; the brackets are actually my pencil marks on the original. My note at the end of her paper read: The sentences in brackets are worth a semester's supply of student papers. "Imperfection does not imply impurity. Impurity is introduced by the way one reacts to imperfection," and "What form of mosaic mind do they possess that allows them to place the pieces into a puzzle whereas the amateurs understand only by reducing the puzzle to pieces?" are examples of Big Talk. Ms. Winsett's mind was obviously focused on ideas, although I'd sent her to the gallery with a thing (shell) in order to describe an event (inspiration) carried out by a person (Barnett Newman). The coach's wife was correct to wonder how a biology professor could use a snail shell and an art museum to get such ideas from a twenty-year-old, stereotypical, all-American athlete on a national championship team. My colleagues could maybe take a lesson from Mrs. Terry Pettit (Anne) and start wondering the same thing, or better yet, start wondering what resources equivalent to a shell and a public museum might be at their fingertips.

In this case, the shell and the particular assignment served as a line of authority beyond which the student had been led. In the zoology courses, which often enrolled 150–200 people, I have used shells numerous times, although in each case the particular assignments varied. Before venturing into such pedagogical territory, a teacher probably needs to answer two questions. The first would be how many different kinds of writing assignments can I give a class with each student focusing on his or her individual shell? And the second would be how might these assignment progress—that is—lead a student down some intellectual path of his or her own choosing, but always toward a common class objective? I honestly believe that my writing assignments cross the paradigmatic authority line found in most university classes and for this reason they free students' minds from certain inhibitions. They know in advance that they must produce something unique and original. They know in advance they will be given repeated opportunities to accomplish this task, and they know that if they do it in one of a million possible ways, they will receive full credit for their efforts. And what they find out after the first paper is graded is that I will ask the most compelling ones to be read publicly.

Public readings may be commonplace in poetry classes, but not necessarily in science classes. Thus when a reading happens, my students discover that it is possible for a science teacher in a large enrollment course to point out the conceptually important parts of their work—in public—without hammering on the picky details or typos. In other words, the authority figure focuses on what's been done right, in the sense of being original and insightful, instead of what's been done wrong, in the sense of not conveying received information (read *text* or *lecture*) accurately. In this case, "right" and "wrong" are not opposites, but instead are qualitatively different attributes of the work. In a public reading, students also discover that the scientist prefers to join them in the audience in order to listen to student ideas, and furthermore, this scientist is more than willing to pass all the accoutrements of authority to a member of the class. I'd be lying if I told you that all students respond positively and productively to such encouragement. There is a great deal of comfort in being subject to authority, in knowing exactly what must be accomplished in order to satisfy a system. But it only takes one individual, one peer, talking Big Talk from the position of power, to open the White Gate.

So, how does one construct a White Gate anywhere, out of anything? Perhaps the image of a steel barrier across some western Nebraska gravel road, materializing out of the midnight darkness in your beat-up truck's headlights, is indeed an appropriate metaphor. The sudden appearance of this gate is a warning that in a few moments, you can no longer conduct business as usual, in this case, simply driving down the road and watching for deer in the bar ditch. A teacher must construct such a barrier that can be seen far enough in advance so that a student realizes a new, or at least different, set of behaviors is about to be required. For the budding scientists who do research in my laboratory, this task proved exceedingly easy, and, in fact, was accomplished by one of them. I had raised the question of how to involve some of the younger researchers, especially the undergraduate women, in the kind of heady, open-ended discussions that often took place among the lubricated guys on late Friday afternoons in Barry's Bar and Grill, a favorite parasitologists' watering hole. Ben Hanelt, a PhD candidate, suggested we set aside an earlier afternoon hour and assemble at The Coffee House, a '50s-aura place a few blocks from campus. The lab would adjourn to coffee at 3:30, talk Big Talk for an hour, then those of legal age could head down to Barry's afterward if they so desired.

This scenario sounds so stupidly simple that even as I write I'm wondering why it's worthy of being included in a *book*. "Go down to The Coffee House for an hour on Friday afternoon and talk" does not sound like something that can revolutionize American higher education. Yet it's been decades since I've seen a group of students and faculty sitting around a table talking, anywhere on my campus, unless forced into the circumstance by some formal arrangement. Yes, I have been invited to scholarship night at the sorority houses, and we do sit at the dinner table and force ourselves to talk about safe subjects for an hour. Yes, I have been invited to similar events in the dorms, and the same kinds of conversations occur except across long tables instead round ones. But since the Vietnam War, in only three places have I regularly seen a table surrounded by students and faculty members talking, just talking Big Talk, among themselves, with everyone participating: Barry's Bar and Grill, the White Gate, and The Coffee House. Of course at the White Gate, the "table" is a pickup bed, but that's certainly no impediment to conversation.

I suppose the Coffee House scenario is worthy of being included in a book about teaching because it's a model of how to produce a

White Gate anywhere. Every week, by Wednesday afternoon, a group of people can "see it coming," and by noon on Friday the members of this group have started putting the brakes on business-as-usual. And by 3:30, by habit, they have shaken off whatever it is that might be constraining the content of their conversation. They've gotten into the habit of physically leaving the lab, where the authority lies with their experiments and a data set. They've gotten into the *habit* of going to coffee *for the express purpose* of talking about something important, something with idea content, something that extends and generalizes their experience of the past week. Periodically they end up talking about people, of course, but even then the line of thought tends to get generalized, for example, from how Professor X treated them, to how Doctor X ought to communicate with Patient Y, to how professionals ought to interact with their peers, period. And in a recapitulation of Hyman Rickover's experience, a discussion that starts with a specific course requirement typically ends with a discussion of the link between the ideal American Way of Life, the evolution of Higher Education, and the development of human resources.

Okay, you say, but half a dozen smart, mature, young honors thesis researchers in The Coffee House is not the same as 200–500 first-year students taking general biology in a multimedia theatre at Big State University. So how do you build, then walk through, a White Gate in a gigantic auditorium? The answer to that question lies in the fact that the podium is *the* symbol of authority. Turn the podium over to your students on a regular basis, and you've led them through the gate. The last time I tried this we used a book. I recently joined two fellow senior faculty members in a rebellion against our local system. If you are a real rebel soldier or renegade politician and by chance are reading this chapter, then we three professors would appreciate it if you would try to laugh politely and discreetly. But when there are four large lecture sections being taught, and three of them use a text different from the fourth, then that fact presents a problem for students who might want to change sections a couple of weeks into the semester. The difference also presents a problem for booksellers, and for lab instructors whose materials are keyed to the different text. But we did it anyway, and furthermore, contracted with a

major publishing house to customize one of its regular texts, eliminating about half the book—the parts not normally covered in the
course—and delivering the text as a paperback. If you ever doubted
how deeply entrenched and conservative higher education can be, try
writing the words "major rebellion" on a three-by-five card and
glancing at this card periodically while you reread this paragraph.
Then remember the old saying that academic politics are so vicious
because there is nothing at stake, nothing, that is, but reputations
resting on ideas.

In addition, however, we compounded this rebellious act by
adding still another text, of supplemental readings, and each of us
chose a different book for this purpose. I chose Lewis Thomas's *Lives
of a Cell*, a book that had captivated my attention when it came out in
the middle 1970s. The other faculty members chose Jonathan
Weiner's, *Beak of the Finch*, and Vincent Dethier's, *To Know a Fly*.
But the question remained what to actually do with these outside
readings? Why have them unless they were used in some meaningful
kind of way? One of the oldest tricks of the teacher trade is to take an
instructor's problem and make it a student's problem. A well-known
version of this trick is to give a quiz when all other attention-getting
devices fail. In this particular semester, this trick worked perfectly. I
simply assigned two of the thirty-two short *Lives* chapters a week to
be reviewed in class, then randomly selected groups of about fifteen
students per week to present, sent them E-mails, encouraged them to
get together, and on Fridays turned the podium over to them.

This act should not strike anyone as particularly creative, rebellious, innovative, or daring. Anyone, that is, except a science professor assigned to teach an introductory course at any large public
university. What did these groups of randomly chosen students do,
and did they accomplish my goals for them? The first question is easy
to answer. They made videotapes and music CDs, devised games,
and acted out skits, all in order to illustrate what they'd learned from
Lewis Thomas. Week after week I sat in the back row, watching
them convey Thomas's magnificent and overreaching ideas about the
technology of medicine, the complexity of infectious diseases, the
value of basic research, and our acceptance of death as a natural
process. But week after week I also watched our Friday audiences

dwindle, and I listened to the "auditorium buzz" increase in volume, especially toward the back of the room. I came to class on Fridays thrilled to be back in the early 1970s, in the company of Vietnam-era student behavior but without the actual war. By the time our randomly selected groups took over the podium, there were names like Nguyen on my roster every semester. But half my students eventually told me, on their evaluations, that our Fridays were a waste of their time.

The idealism that drives the kinds of experiments I've just described is sometimes difficult to sustain, especially in an educational enterprise trying to run itself like a business. If you open a shop and half your potential customers believe it's a waste of time coming through the door, then you're on the road to bankruptcy. But teaching is not a business. Neither is learning. In an educational enterprise, if you don't force your customers to struggle with ideas, to walk up Oliver Wendell Holmes' stairs no matter how much they'd rather stay on the first floor, then as a teacher you've failed. And if you don't purposefully try to lead as many as you can through that White Gate then you've failed a society that still cannot live up to Hyman Rickover's hopes and expectations and Eleanor Roosevelt's visions of a civilized world.

12

BUILDING EDEN

Old habits die hard.
Deborah Meier (from *The Power of Their Ideas*)

The Biblical Garden of Eden is our western symbol of the original, biologically diverse, and unspoiled Earth onto which innocent human beings were placed. Although we now tend to think of Africa's Rift Valley, running from Syria into Mozambique, as a literal Garden of Eden—that is, the "birthplace" of humanity—we nevertheless use the "Eden" idea to denote blissful times in some relative paradise. Nebraska's mud, worms, and microscopes may not translate into "bliss" and "paradise" for everyone, but we all have our visions of the ideal environment in which to conduct our business. And when we're not plunked down in that environment, then we must build it, largely from our intellectual endeavors and values.

Remember that in Eden, everything a teacher needs is right at his or her fingertips, all in proper context, a rich supply of wonder for every student, and all of it "alive," if not literally—for a biologist—then figuratively for the artist, historian, economist, musician. This supply of wonder in our immediate environment, once perceived as such, is suddenly revealed to occur all around us and in such profusion that a teacher must become a student in order to utilize it. When we started the Cedar Point Biological Station, the place was just one more collection of abandoned buildings out on the prairie a million miles from home. When we had to deliver an educational enterprise then we started looking more closely at our surroundings, places most people would consider little more than pasture and a typical prairie river. The biologists who built this castle were not "most people"; they were teachers first and foremost, and they were separated from all the standard materials used by teachers everywhere. For us in the mid-1970s, the construction of Eden was almost entirely a mental activity, although having ready access to marshes and prairies cer-

tainly made such a synthesis easier than it might have been otherwise. Nevertheless, the building of an ideal school, in the very broad-
est sense, still is, and likely always will be, any time and anywhere,
first and foremost, an accomplishment of the unfettered mind.

The major tool for building such a learning place is little more
than a willingness to see any and every element of one's social and
physical environment as material, no matter what the subject. Math-
ematicians, artists, poets, scientists, philosophers, historians, or even
economists can all use a single leaf as a lecture or laboratory subject—
if they'll just figure out how to do it. Every teacher knows this assertion is true; few have the time, patience, training, and courage to let
such knowledge direct their practice. But when a single small ———
can be used by ——— to engage young people in an activity that
provides transferable skills, insight, and intellectual maturity, then
the castle is finished and the doors are opened. All you have to do
now is keep out the termites. By "termites" I mean all those factors
that slowly work their way into and through whatever enterprise
we've started, factors such as habit, narrowing vision, fatigue, administrative accountability, frustration, stress. The Queen Termite, the
source of all those workers eating away at your paradise, is the feeling
that we're not doing something of value unless we impress the accountants—both the literal and the metaphorical ones.

In higher education, where faculty members have so much freedom in the classroom, those very same faculty members are also
often the accountants least worthy of our efforts to impress. In other
words, we are by and large our own worst enemies. We are quick to
criticize colleagues who do not toe the paradigmatic party line, we
are extraordinarily conservative in matters of curricular change, we
resent our friends' creativity, and we wear our insecurities on our
sleeves. Eventually, we take out our frustrations on our students.
Nary a university department exists that does not subject itself to pe-
riodic self-scrutiny, often at the instigation of outside reviewers, and
usually because we get tired of fighting among ourselves. Such intro-
spective research often results in an altered curriculum, and the
whole cycle begins anew. The previously mentioned dean who prided
himself on having "gotten rid of the −ologies" is a perfect summary of
this kind of process at work. One of my senior colleagues character-

ized our most recent revisions as "old wine in new bottles," and of course he is right.

Often the driving force in this revision (recycling) is the feeling that we're not "modern," not keeping up with the cutting edge, not incorporating the latest ideas, technologies, and discoveries, not mentioning the latest piece of wondrous research to hit the journals. This feeling derives from the belief that content is more important than what you actually ask your class to do. For example, we might assert that for a student, knowing the ultrastructure of an ameba is more important than what you do with knowledge of protistan morphology, ultra or not. This idea is somewhat akin to the one that it's more important to know that Picasso painted *Les Demoiselles d'Avignon* in 1907 than it is to understand how and why an individual, almost single-handedly, could invent cubism. Or for that matter, to believe that being able to list the cubists and their productive periods is more important than to further understand what effect Picasso's invention had on our general perception of the world.

Of course twenty professors will sit in a faculty meeting and assuredly declare that you have to do both—learn content as well as process—because you can't understand one without the other. And, of course, these twenty professors are right. The argument will be over whether to start with content and continue to process, or to start with process as a reason for acquiring content. This argument is really one over whether to focus on the material for its own sake— that is, to define content *as* the subject—or on the material as a vehicle for teaching transferable skills. If the former, then we can never get enough material; if the latter, then we don't need nearly as much material because the student will be able to transfer his or her information-processing skills to new subjects as these are encountered. I have yet to see an instance in which process wins out over material except at the individual level. This is why some teachers and their students seem to be so successful and productive in spite of their apparent ignorance while other teachers and students seem to be so unsuccessful in spite of their apparent knowledge.

As a thought experiment to illustrate this assertion, envision a go-around-the-room exercise in which each student is asked to come up with a different educational use for the single leaf mentioned on p. 162. In this type of exercise, everyone tacitly agrees there are no "right answers," only interesting suggestions. You hand this leaf to the first person, and ask that she come up with an idea for a whole biology lab exercise for herself and a partner using only this one leaf. Then she passes the leaf to the next person, who is asked to tell the class how he would use that same item for a three-hour physics lab. From there on, the rest of the students come up with their own ideas for use of this leaf in an afternoon's exercise on art, on music, poetry, fiction, history, mathematics, business. Is this sort of an exercise educational? I believe so, but then not everyone would agree. If you were in that room, however, taking careful notes on what these students were saying, then you'd have your roadmap to Eden. That map is simply the decision that whatever is at hand, essentially free and readily available, items you can pick up as easily as you can that fallen leaf, is yours to use as instructional material. Once this decision is made, you have suddenly switched your focus from content to process, and in doing so you have made the former subordinate to the latter.

This dichotomy in our own view of our job as teachers—purveyors of content and paradigm versus process and breadth—is at the heart of many of our most heated, divisive, and destructive internal academic battles. The two opposing views, and the different practices they inspire, are, in my opinion, only surface manifestations of a previously mentioned conflict—namely—rebellion against the authority of paradigm. In other words, we're talking about conservatives versus liberals. The academic political fallout from this contest is quite asymmetrical. Liberals' failures often get magnified into an image of incompetence, but liberals usually don't really care much what conservatives think and do, or whether they fail or succeed. I strongly suspect that there exists in every academic department, of every discipline, at least in every secular college or university, a pair of faculty members who typify these different approaches to intellectual life. Although obviously I'm a liberal, I don't necessarily believe the conservatives are always evil. The ones I've watched, however, seem to be unhappy a lot of the time, apparently because they can't figure out why the liberals' students seem to be so successful. My suggestion to anyone bewildered by the ultimate success of certain young people should look up the definition of "transferable skills," or maybe reassess the fundamental value of a broad education. I contend that the arts and sciences ideals—breadth of understanding, courage to explore anywhere, patience with disagreement—are the best antidotes to our current afflictions of banality, specialization, and information overload.

How much Eden should be built into a typical university classroom? Perhaps surprisingly, having just presented a utopian advertisement for the liberal arts, I believe the answer is some, but not too much. For example, in order to be certified in many disciplines, a student must acquire and demonstrate specified skills. You don't want to drive over a bridge designed by an engineer who spent his entire undergraduate career contemplating a single leaf, and indeed that student would not graduate from any engineering college on this planet. But eventually you might want to live in a house built from recycled plastics woven into exceptionally strong sheets and tubes whose basic design was inspired by the structure of plant cell walls. You wouldn't trust your tax return to an accountant who'd spent four years at State U doing little more than counting leaves on campus trees. You might, however, want to discuss your taxes with an accountant who had not only learned his spreadsheets and laws, but who had also studied the interconnectedness of various systems far beyond the business world. Such an accountant might well be able to see, and articulate, legitimate relationships between some of your expenditures and your income-generating activities, relationships that others might easily miss. The systems could be anything from tropical forests to New York traffic. If the former, a teacher could certainly begin one class with a leaf, if the latter, an ignition key might suffice as the launching pad.

The only real danger this teacher faces is the self-delusion that accompanies power. It's easy to start believing we're great, when, in fact, about all we're doing is something akin to what Cro-Magnon shamans must have done: build a universe from materials at hand. The only things that keep such delusion at bay are natural forces over which one has no control. Thus ideal teachers are under constant pressure to select from an enormous supply of materials in order to construct a conceptually significant experience for students and themselves. This process is exactly the opposite of what university professors normally do. In general, most of us eliminate vast quantities of materials from our realm of consciousness simply because we don't have time to understand them. In other words, we specialize because we have to in order to do research and publish. But we don't have to specialize in order to fulfill our teaching obligations, those responsibilities we have not only to our employers, but also—more important—to our society and our species.

If the preceding paragraph sounds somewhat academic, then put yourself in my shoes for a moment and I'll explain what it means by comparing two different approaches to a teaching situation. Imagine yourself at Cedar Point about to take a field trip to the North Platte River south of a small town called Lewellen, Nebraska. What are you going to do on this trip? The answer depends on two things: your subject and your approach. Let's say the subject is parasitology. What kinds of approaches could we take? An obvious one—the first in our example—would be to seine fish, put them in a bucket, take them back to the laboratory, dissect them, collect the parasites, make slides, identify the worms, then follow that activity in a couple of days with a test. Would the students learn something about parasites from doing such an exercise? Of course. Such an exercise would be quite valuable for no reason than that the students themselves had developed the set of materials over which they would be tested, rather than bought these materials at the bookstore.

Alternatively, however, we could plan for something more than a collecting trip followed by a test over the results—namely the second approach. In addition to simply collecting fish, we could spend an hour or two on fish identification and minnow demography, we could break up into groups and explore the diverse sections of the river to discover if each held a different fish community, and we could collect some invertebrates—leeches, crustaceans, aquatic insects, snails—from those same sites. These invertebrates are the intermediate hosts for—that is, the sources of—many parasites in the fish. We could stand in the middle of the river and talk about water-rights issues, legal battles between states, and massive impoundments upstream. We could have a mud fight, although every time that happens I imagine the university's lawyers glaring over my shoulder. We could stop for a short lesson on aquatic vegetation, its taxonomy, ecology, and geographic distribution. Having anticipated the extra time needed for these additional activities, we would have packed a great lunch with lots of cookies, made from scratch in the Cedar Point kitchen. We would thus be prepared for a picnic in a nearby state park, where we could sit around the tables and talk about Native American artifacts found in the cliffs above us and Gold Rush–era wagon ruts still visible on a nearby hill.

Back at the field station we could take an hour's break for a shower and a thirty-minute nap, then spend the next three or four hours dissecting, videotaping, counting, and measuring parasites, making tissue smears, fixing worms for later permanent slide preparation, and sharing one another's discoveries. After dinner we could analyze our data. We could spend a couple of more hours discussing the results, playing go-around-the-room, and using all our river lessons to speculate on the factors dictating "who's infected with whom." Then we could clean up the lab, adjourn to the White Gate or some local watering hole, and continue the discussion. Late into the evening we could talk about projects that might be done using fish parasites in the North Platte River, students who have done such projects in the past, and where they are now. Over the next day or two, my graduate students could help the undergrads work through problems in specimen preparation. I know from experience that this extended and multifaceted approach to a prairie river sticks with students for years, even as their detailed knowledge of microscopic worms fades into oblivion.

In the first of these field trips, the instructor has ignored everything but the items of immediate interest. By doing this, he or she has imposed a personal order on nature, and the students' experience reflects that imposition. Textbooks use this approach out of necessity, but sometimes try to provide context with short essays. A good example of this technique would be the few paragraphs on, plus a picture of, Henrietta Lacks, the donor of Hela cells, that one sometimes finds in chapters on cell structure. Routinely, however, throughout a typical biology text, context is discarded for a focus on some narrow subject. But in the second field trip, time is taken to build context, to surround the subject with knowledge of those factors that influence it. Furthermore, time is budgeted to assimilate the often-complex interactions, either revealed or hypothesized, between the subject and its environment. The first approach is by far the easiest one. Furthermore, students seem to appreciate the apparent organization. Thus any teacher who uses the second approach must also train his or her students to use it, must be patient with the frustration that often develops when student are first exposed to such teaching, and must constantly provide positive support to those students who successfully take even small steps.

Not everyone has a North Platte River nearby to use as a classroom, although few of us do have art museums, which tend to share certain characteristics with braided prairie rivers. That is, such museums are highly heterogeneous environments; themes such as interdependency are typically manifested in numerous ways; and, their objects are heavily infused with historical and social content. Thus it is no surprise that I constantly use the University of Nebraska Sheldon Memorial Art Gallery in the same way I use the environment around Cedar Point. I send students in there on seemingly impossible assignments, but at the same time give them total freedom to complete these assignments in any of a thousand different ways. Billie Jean Winsett's "The Light Not on the Horizon" was an excellent example of such integrative adventures. Compare that essay, however, with the one that follows shortly, and you will see instantly how any rich source of imagery can be used over and over again in various ways, and without consuming it. Suddenly we are no longer talking about specific assignments and their results, but about the visual literacy required to understand biology—that is—one of the central pedagogical issues in science education.

The following essay was written by a student named Heather Easter, and it was submitted on November 12, 1999, in response to an assignment in Biological Sciences 101, a class with 265 students. I had asked them to choose five pieces, in three different media, in the Sheldon Gallery. These mainly first-year students were then to tell me in three double-spaced pages how these pieces of art illustrated "The Big Picture in Biology." Admittedly, when a professor is trying to sell his or her grand ideas about teaching, that prof. does not choose the worst of 265 freshman papers to illustrate these ideas. So Ms. Easter's work can be considered close to the ideal. Nevertheless, sometimes the results of our innovative approaches show us what is possible, and such demonstrations help us weather the criticism and failure that routinely accompany innovation. Thus I will admit to having read this essay almost as many times as I have read "Who Gives a Shell?" and "The Light Not on the Horizon." Here is Heather's essay reprinted with her permission; it seemed to me in November, 1999, that she got the point and used her material well, and it still seems that way to me. As with Billie Jean Winsett's papers, I recommend resisting any stupid impulse to edit; the world is full of "editors" and like Ms. Winsett, Ms. Easter will encounter them soon enough, if she has not done so already.

After looking around the Sheldon Gallery, I decided to focus on five particular pieces of artwork for this assignment. In order to tie in artwork with "The Big Picture in Biology," I examined a diverse range of work. The first piece I noted was Albert Bierstadt's *River Landscape*, which is an outstanding painting of nature including pine trees, a lake, birds, the moon, tall cliffs, and the shadow of a deer in the lake water. Next, I examined Deborah Butterfield's sculpture *Derby Horse*, which is a creative interpretation of a horse made out of rust, metal, and nails. The next piece of artwork I looked at, Charles Rain's *Lichen Document*, included several biologically significant creatures such as a type of spotted moth or butterfly, moss and lichens growing on a decaying branch, and a peculiar winged insect. Ansel Easton Adams' print entitled *The Tetons and the Snake River, Grand Teton National Park, Wyoming* displayed magnificent snow-covered mountains with the Snake River winding through the trees under a cloudy sky with rays of sunshine peaking through. Finally, I noticed William Henry Jackson's *Gateway at the Garden of the Gods, Near Manitou*, which is a black-and-white print of nature including tall mountains and cliffs, dark trees, and barren land spotted with cactus.

After thinking about all that I have learned about biological diversity thus far, I was reminded of the class discussion on life's hierarchy of organization and how organisms interact with an ecosystem in order to survive. An ecosystem includes all living and nonliving organisms living in a particular area that interact with one another for survival. The word survival is also an important word in biology. From Darwin's idea of natural selection to the study of evolution, inherited change in organisms over time, biological diversity has been created. The various pieces of artwork mentioned above can be integrated together to show just how biologically diverse an ecosystem is.

The two pieces of artwork entitled *River Landscape* and *The Tetons and the Snake River, Grand Teton National Park, Wyoming* represent one type of ecosystem that includes a body of water that the community of organisms builds its living environment around. One piece of art portrays a lake and the other a winding river, but the representation can be described as similar. Many diverse populations of trees are evident in these pieces of art. I noticed pine trees, trees without leaves, large oak trees, and also smaller trees inhabited by small animals. In life's hierarchy of organization, underneath the population is the organism level. As I looked at the two representations of nature, I saw a population of birds. On the organism level, a shadow of a deer was evident in the lake water of Bierstadt's *River Landscape*.

If I were to analyze this deer even farther down in life's hierarchy of organization, next I would look at the organ system level of the deer. Just like humans, deer have organ systems such as a circulatory system, a nervous system, and a digestive system, just to name a few. After the organ system comes the organ level in which each organ system contains individual organs. The deer has organs such as a brain, a stomach, and a heart. Using the deer's heart as an example, the organ is next made up of different tissues, which have specific functions that enable the heart to pump a continuous blood supply to the other organs in the deer's body. The deer's heart tissues are made of individual cells. Finally, after the cellular level comes the molecular level. A molecule is a group of atoms. This breakdown of organization in an ecosystem is an example of biological diversity, and these two pieces of artwork capture the very essence of the various levels of biological life.

William Henry Jackson's *Gateway at the Garden of the Gods, Near Manitou* represents a different type of biological ecosystem, which is also a great example of the bigger picture of biology. This landscape seems to be more of a barren and dry climate ecosystem. The mountains, cliffs, and dry land all make up the area in which organisms live. The community level includes all of the organisms living in this particular ecosystem. Various populations of trees and cactus were evident. Although this particular piece did not have any visible animals or insects in it, I am sure that several living organisms occupy the land that have adapted to that particular dry environment such as lizards and maybe even camels. One living organism that stood out in this piece of artwork was a cactus. A cactus is made of cells, and tissues, and atoms just like the deer mentioned above. The fact that the cactus has to adapt to its environment, which does not contain a large supply of water in order to survive is of much biological significance. This is also an example of evolution.

So far I have described large ecosystems with numerous populations of organisms living in them, but an ecosystem can also be very small in size. This is evident in Charles Rain's *Lichen Document*. It is fascinating that a painting of just one tree branch inhabited by living organisms can represent everything from the ecosystem level down to the molecular level of life. This is a true representation of biology working together to survive among predators, aversive weather conditions, and limited food supply. The single branch is covered in lichens and moss and is inhabited by a spotted moth, a distinct winged insect, and other small insects and organisms that make up the community. The community, in turn, is made up of individual organisms. The spotted moth caught my attention right away. Its wings have adapted the organism to be mobile in order to find food and shelter to survive in its environment. The moth is also made up of organs, tissues, cells, and molecules. The main difference in this particular piece of art is the intricate detail of biological diversity all found on one tree branch.

The final piece of art that can be tied into the bigger picture of biological diversity is Deborah Butterfield's sculpture *Derby Horse*. Beginning at the organism level, the horse is an example of evolution in this nation's history. This single organism is made up of various organ systems such as the nervous, circulatory, and digestive system, for example. On the organ level the horse has a brain. The brain is made of numerous tissues that have specialized function in the brain. The brain tissues consist of millions of cells and the cells are made of molecules. No matter where you look in biology, every organism can be broken down into its component parts. This biological phenomenon can help us to learn more about the structure and functions of life on earth.

I would never have thought that going to the Sheldon Art Gallery would have given me any insight into how biology diversity is represented in everyday life. This assignment opened my eyes to just how much the liberal arts can be applied to something as scientific as life's hierarchy of organization. I chose to compare these particular pieces of artwork to the bigger picture of biology, because they were each unique. At the same time, they could all be related to one main theme in biology. Now I am beginning to understand just how much biology affects my everyday life.

The idea for this assignment came out of a conversation with another faculty member—Ted Pardy, winner of my university's highest teaching award—about survey data concerning student reaction to biological science classes. I don't remember the circumstances of our conversation, or the source of these data. I do remember the essence and the result, however. The survey indicated that students felt they were learning lots of facts and details, but rarely got exposed to the big picture. Ted and I talked awhile about this particular problem and how it might be resolved. We didn't come to any startling conclusions, but as a result of that discussion I did decide to send Ms. Easter and her 264 classmates to the art museum. I could, of course, have just given a couple of lectures on "The Big Picture in Biology" and called it quits. In fact, I do that periodically. After those lectures, I usually go back to the lab and do research, expecting to eventually write three or four multiple-choice questions on The Big Picture. As part of their BioSci 101 experience, however, Heather Easter and her classmates spent at least 300 person-hours (about eight weeks of full-time work, collectively) in an art museum. Then they gave me nearly 800 pages of student writing to read, all on the subject "The Big Picture in Biology" as seen in the products of 200+ well-known artists. That's why I'm able to resist the temptation to edit their papers very much.

What would I do if I were a professor of English instead of invertebrate zoology? Where is that intellectual paradise for a teacher of modern fiction? Of poetry? And once I find it, how do I take its pedagogical power and give that power to my students? I'm going to step beyond my bounds and try to answer these questions, then step even further beyond those bounds and try to answer them for history, economics, engineering, music, and art. I believe that along with literature and science, these five fields encompass all of the basic domains of reality found in human scholarly endeavor. I don't have a professional's, or a professor's, knowledge of these seven disciplines. But if, with respect to these seven areas of intellectual pursuits, we ask the following questions: What is a fact? What is an observation? What evidence do we need in order to make a decision? How do we interpret information? What use do humans make of our products? And what is the fundamental nature of prevailing paradigms? Then the answers will tell us most of what we need to know to build Eden.

Acknowledgments

I would like to personally thank everyone who has contributed to this book and to the ideas and experiences related in these pages. Foremost among these individuals are not only the students whose work I've used, always with their permission, but also all the other nearly 13,000 students whose writing I've read for the past thirty-six years. Among these thousands of people are some that were not the least bit happy with what I'd asked them to do, and quite a few others who approached their assigned tasks without discernable enthusiasm. But there were plenty whose entire vision of their surroundings, and their place in those surroundings, were dramatically changed because they'd been asked to help build an ideal place for their minds to dwell. These are the people who validated my choice to ask them to do something unusual.

I also need to give my deepest and most sincere thanks to the University of Nebraska and the people of Nebraska. Although it sounds pretty corny, I've been treated quite well by this state, and feel as if I have lived a life of extreme privilege as a result of that decision, in the spring of 1966, to accept my first faculty position at a salary of $8,600 per year. The University of Nebraska coughed up the money to start the Cedar Point Biological Station, and continued, throughout most of my career, to dump money into the program, although in modest amounts. The students who came to CPBS were often a little bit uncertain about what they'd gotten themselves into, but virtually to a person, by the time their summer experience was over, they were enthusiastic field biologists well acquainted with the "real stuff." I greatly appreciate their help and enthusiasm. The first CPBS director, Brent Nickol, was an exceedingly skillful and efficient administrator without whom the field program would probably not have survived. Gary Hergenrader, a faculty member in the School of Natural Resources, provided the information about Roger Macklem.

The ranchers in western Nebraska have contributed beyond description to my professional development, and to my understanding—as yet incomplete—of the process of education. At least six families: the Dunwoodys, the Sillasens, the Haythorns, the Thalkens, the Petersons, and the McGinleys, have each given the University of Nebraska the equivalent of a laboratory and classroom building filled with supplies and specimens, although to them that laboratory looked more like ponds, creeks, rivers, and well tanks than like rooms with fume hoods, sterile benches, and strange glassware. The Gainsforth family, original owners of the land upon which Cedar Point is located, have always been strong supporters of the program. Myrna Gainsforth provided the story of Silas P. (p. 18) and the original homestead. Betty Dowling's letter was provided by her husband, Phil, who was the first facilities manager at CPBS. Both Betty and Phil are deceased. The inescapable conclusion is that simply by living their own lives in the places their family histories had taken them, these western Nebraska folks ended up providing gifts of staggering value. I never would have known any of these families had CPBS not been established and had I not volunteered to teach out there. At the end of a career, when one counts his blessings, the generosity of these ranchers must be right there near the top of the list.

I constantly use the two museums on my campus as teaching resources. Three directors played major roles in building and maintaining the natural history museum facilities and exhibits that we now use: Erwin Barbour, Bertrand Schultz, and Hugh Genoways, although the museum artists: Elizabeth Dolan, Nathan Moller, and Marc Marcuson actually produced much of the visual imagery that is so vital to the educational mission. The Sheldon Memorial Art Gallery is also a major museum, specializing in twentieth century American art. Norman Geske and George Neubert are the directors largely responsible for assembling the collection as now stands. My wife Karen is the Curator of Education at the Sheldon, and through her I have gained a great appreciation for artists, art historians, art education, and the singular value of works of art.

I also am deeply indebted to the students who have allowed their work and their names to be used in this book, although I did not use all of their material for which I was granted permission. These students include: Wendy Allen, Heidi Baumert, Adam Brosz, Meredith Carpenter, Megan Collins, Jillian Detwiler, Laura Duclos, Katie Easley, Heather Easter, Michelle Fischbach, Laura Grother, Andrew Lund, Karen Pearson Miller, Ashley Selig, Todd Spohn, Sara Strongin, Kristin Vavrina, Billie Jean Winsett Fletcher, and Sara Zulkoski. The Novak family (chapter 1) actually consists of two families I interviewed in the past five years; the dialogue is pretty much verbatim but the names were changed to protect identities. Similarly, the letter of recommendation is a combination of two such letters written over the past decade, although one or more of the statements in it have been included in at least a hundred such letters. The student's name in that letter is not real, although Jackie O'Hara is the actual UNMC administrator who receives these letters.

References

Adler, M. J. 1982. *The Paideia Proposal: An Educational Manifesto*. New York: Macmillan.

Arsuaga, J. L. 2001. *The Neanderthal's Necklace: In Search of the First Thinkers*. New York: Four Walls Eight Windows. (Translation, 2002.)

Balzar, J. 2002. "Information Age Has Killed Curiosity." *Lincoln Journal-Star*, November 6. (Reprinted from the *Los Angeles Times*.)

Berlinski, D. 2002. "What Brings a World Into Being?" In: *The Best Science Writing 2002*. Ed. M. Ridley, New York: HarperCollins.

Brant, Sara. 1999. Personal communication. The comment about sources of projects (chapter 8) by Sara Brant, a graduate student at the University of Nebraska, was made after her return from the joint meetings of the Society for the Study of Evolution, the American Society of Naturalists, and the Society of Systematic Biologists, in Madison, Wisconsin, in 1999.

Cavalli-Sforza, L. L., and M. W. Feldman. 1981. *Cultural Transmission and Evolution: A Quantitative Approach*. Princeton: Princeton University Press.

Collins, M. R., and J. Janovy, Jr. 2003. "Host Specificity Among Ancyrocephalinae (Monogenoidea) of Nebraska Sunfish." *Journal of Parasitology* 89:80–83.

Fussell, P. 1989. *Wartime: Understanding and Behavior in the Second World War*. New York: Oxford University Press.

Hofstadter, D. 1985. *Metamagical themas: Questing for the Essence of Mind and Pattern*. New York: Basic Books.

Holmes, O. W. 1891. *The Poet at the Breakfast Table: He Talks with His Fellow Boarders and the Reader*. Boston: Houghton, Mifflin.

Kuhn, T. H. 1996. *The Structure of Scientific Revolutions*, 2nd Ed. Chicago: University of Chicago Press.

Kubey, R., and M. Csikszentmihalyi. 2001. "Television Addiction Is No Mere Metaphor." *Scientific American* 286:74–80.

MacArthur, R. H., and E. O. Wilson. 1967. *The Theory of Island Biogeography*. Princeton: Princeton University Press.

Meier, D. 1995. *The Power of Their Ideas: Lessons for America from a Small School in Harlem*. Boston: Beacon Press.

Milosz, C. 2001. *To Begin Where I Am: Selected Essays*. New York: Farrar, Straus and Giroux.

Moore, J. A. 1993. *Science as a Way of Knowing: the Foundations of Modern Biology*. Cambridge: Harvard University Press.

National Arts Education Consortium (no date). "Transforming Arts Education Through the Arts Challenge: Final Project Report." Department of Art Education. Columbus: Ohio State University.

Nixon, A. F. 1949. *Teaching Biology for Appreciation: Techniques and Materials for Teaching Biology Contributing toward its Appreciation and Correlation with Art, Literature and Social Studies*. Boston: Chapman and Grimes.

Parks, R., and J. Haskins. 1992. *Rosa Parks: My Story*. New York: Dial Books.

Power, S. 2002. *"A Problem from Hell": America and the Age of Genocide*. New York: Basic Books.

Slobodkin, L. 1992. *Simplicity and Complexity in Games of the Intellect*. Cambridge: Harvard University Press.

Stevenson, B. (Ed.) 1967. *The Home Book of Quotations*. New York: Dodd, Mead.

Weichman, M. A., and J. Janovy, Jr. 1999. "Parasite Community Structure in *Pimephales promelas* (Pisces: Cyprinidae) from Two Converging Streams." *Journal of Parasitology*, 86:654–656.

Wilson, B. 1997. *The Quiet Evolution: Changing the Face of Arts Education*. Los Angeles: The Getty Education Institute for the Arts.

Wilson, E. O. 1978. *On Human Nature*. Cambridge: Harvard University Press.

Index

*For Product Safety Concerns and Information please contact
our EU representative GPSR@taylorandfrancis.com Taylor & Francis
Verlag GmbH, Kaufingerstraße 24, 80331 München, Germany*

T - #0133 - 270225 - C0 - 229/152/11 - PB - 9780415946674 - Gloss Lamination